The Adamant Co-op Cookbook

Recipes, stories, and more compiled and
edited by volunteers and staff of the
Adamant Cooperative, Inc., Adamant, Vermont

Vermont's and the Nation's* Oldest Cooperative Food Store

Featuring the works of artist Janet MacLeod

*According to Knupfer, Anne Meis: Food Coops in America: Communities, Consumption, and Economic Democracy. 2013, Cornell University, p. 11, the Adamant Cooperative is the oldest food cooperative in the United States.

ISBN 978-0-692-46982-8

Printed by L. Brown & Sons Printing, Inc., Barre, Vermont, USA

The hamlet of Adamant, Vermont, was originally named Sodom. In fact, the hamlet stands today at the edge of Sodom Pond. The story goes that long ago a group of concerned residents, well aware of the Biblical implications of the name, went to their legislators and expressed their adamant desire that the name of Sodom be changed. And so it was.

That spirit of involvement in and concern about community lived on, and the residents of Adamant went on to do some amazing things.

This book is dedicated to the founding members of the Adamant Cooperative, Inc., and to the memory of Lois Toby (1926-2015), who was here through thick and thin.

Contents

Poetry, Essays

ACKNOWLEDGEMENTS

For our 75th anniversary, we invited the community to a brunch -- to thank everybody for their support of our Co-op. It was a beautiful July morning, lots of people came, talked, and enjoyed the food offered. This was when we hatched the idea of a book for our 80th anniversary. It had to be beautiful and special -- hey -- after all, we had five years to work on it!

Well, four years passed. We occasionally mentioned our 80th anniversary. Talked of a book. Okay, so maybe we didn't do that much in four years, but we did know that we wanted to make a cookbook with lots of art in it -- an art cookbook. The next thing we knew, the 80th anniversary was looming and panic set in.

Having this book ready to go to the printer feels great. This book is truly a labor of love -- everybody who contributed to it donated their talent, time, ideas or "just" a recipe. We want to thank everybody in Adamant, "greater" Adamant, and all honorary citizens of Adamant who contributed.

As is almost always the case in a project such as this, a few people did the lion's share of the work. This book would be nothing without Janet MacLeod's artwork -- you can see it on almost every single page of this book.Her paintings and drawings make it special. Her style speaks to so many of us and her ability seemingly to whip out painting after painting inspired the rest of us to keep going.

Larry Floersch thought that he could just enjoy retirement -- we thought otherwise. We found our ideal editor: somebody who actually was an editor in his former life, who is an amazing chef, and who has a great sense of humor. Lucky for us, Larry came on board and made sense of all the papers we threw at him.

Janet Wass is not only a great presence at the Co-op, she also has a keen eye for detail and for how to make things look beautiful. She asked the right questions and spent hours moving pictures and recipes around until they were just right. We never question her judgement -- because it always turns out that she is right anyway.

And as you see, we pulled it together. We are very proud of our little book. It is amazing what we can accomplish when we all work together. We hope you enjoy it for a long time to come. All proceeds from this book benefit the Adamant Co-op. We also hope that you come and visit us -- grab some coffee and fresh scones; pick up a few groceries; tell us about your latest trip; complain about your children, parents, or neighbors; or share a book or movie recommendation. We look forward to welcoming you at the Co-op.

And tell your family and friends about us -- who knows what stroke of genius we will come up with for our 100th anniversary?

Regina Thompson, March 2015

Introduction

by Eva Gumprecht

We hope that the recipes in this book will help you make some wonderful meals. When push comes to shove, the recipes are not so much about measurements and techniques or perfection of presentation as they are about story and connection: stories of community, history, meals shared, food offered to a sick neighbor, given in celebration, in mourning, in the depth of winter, the height of summer. They come from a sense of plenty. They are steeped in memory and relationship. The central ingredient is generosity, the desire to feed each other.

The hub of this cookbook is the Adamant Co-op, a tiny store that acts as the center and magnet for a web of community which transcends any geographic boundaries. Quite a few of us moved here because of the Co-op. Because entering its doors touched something in us, a sense of people mattering to each other, of quirkiness, of space for human ingredients to find a place in this beautiful, messy stew of life.

The recipes, like any human community, are varied and ever-evolving. Sometimes sophisticated, sometimes rough, sometimes precise, sometimes loose, some invented yesterday, some many generations old. All of them are here because they gave people pleasure.

Some are favorites at the Adamant Co-op Friday night

Cookouts. Some fly out the store as carpenters stop for their morning muffins, or writers needing a touch of human interaction come for a piping hot empanada, or young parents coming back from work in town too tired to make dinner pick up soup to heat at home.

The recipes have been carried in baskets to potlucks, left on neighbors' doorsteps, kept cold on winter porches, shielded from mud season splatter. This is cooking in the midst of life and chaos, kids, imperfect bodies, and

memories. And sometimes the simple childhood tastes just can't be topped. Among this health-conscious, organic crowd our top seller, at cookouts, is a jumbo hot dog, nitrates, nitrites, and all. Often ordered sheepishly with a whispered "I only eat these here."

When life hands you a flaming wooden door from the pizza oven, you run to the brook with it. When a child stares into the glowing depths of the pizza oven and asks if there's going to be dessert, the S'More pizza, with chocolate chips and marshmallows, is born. Some of the best recipes arose when the larder was missing essential ingredients and so there was no choice but to improvise. We hope that you will continue the tradition and make them your own.

As well as eating together at the summer Friday Night Cookouts, dead-of-winter evenings of Decadent Desserts (it turns out there really is such a thing as too much chocolate!), fall-foliage Mad Woodchuck's Tea Parties, or the infamous Black Fly Festival, the Co-op is a place for cooking and creating together.

Making this cookbook has been a great excuse to hang out in each others' kitchens, sample vast amounts of delicious food (how could we pass it along to you unless we knew it was really good?), peek in the studio upstairs as Janet paints one beautiful illustration after another. May it bring you as much warmth and connection as it has brought us.

A Short History of The Co-op

by Scott Thompson

The Adamant Cooperative at 80

On August 1, 1935, under the urging and leadership of Rev. Raymond Ebbett, pastor of the Adamant Methodist Church, and after many months of study and experimentation, Adamant residents opened the first consumer cooperative in the state of Vermont. After 80 years, it remains the oldest cooperative food store in Vermont, and, according to one source, is the oldest in the United States.*

Historian Weston A. Cate, Jr. (in the book "Forever Calais") described the new-born institution: "Thirty-nine members bought $5 shares, and with this working capital the co-op rented the store operated by Mrs. Minnie Horr and purchased her stock in trade. Her store, originally a boarding house for quarry workers, is the same building where the Adamant Co-op is located [today]."

Consumer cooperatives are not typically so long-lived. One can understand why. Consumer co-ops tend to coalesce out of an extraordinary burst of desperation or revolt against the failings of an existing system for distributing goods. During the Great Depression of the 1930s,

* Knupfer, Anne Meis: Food Coops in America: Communities, Consumption, and Economic Democracy. 2013, Cornell University, p. 11.

desperation and revolt often occurred together, making this otherwise dismal period a golden age for cooperatives. The Adamant Co-op outlived its origins, survived, and even came to thrive in its own way. Through its various evolutions, the Co-op has in some ways come full circle. As Janet MacLeod put it, "At the start, people in Adamant bought from each other because they had to. Now we buy from each other because we want to."

The Years of Expansion

The initial success of its cooperative model inspired Adamant residents with the zeal and ambition to tackle other aspects of economic life where the existing system had failed, as well as to extend the cooperative idea more broadly.

Electricity came first. Residents formed another study group that ultimately led to the creation of the Washington Electric Cooperative in 1939. Wes Cate writes, "The first three presidents of the electric co-op ... had also been directors of the Adamant co-op." Today, the Washington Electric Cooperative serves over 10,000 members, 97% of whom are residential consumers.

Then finance. Via the same process of study groups and patient laying of groundwork, a collection of residents including Rev. Ebbett, drew up by-laws for a credit union in late 1941. The Adamant Credit Union became the first in Vermont to be chartered on February 12, 1942, under a new state law on credit unions.

Finally came Maple Corner, four miles up County Road. When the Maple Corner Store was put up for sale in 1945, the members of the Adamant Co-op voted to buy it. For the next 28 years, through fire (1947) and flood (1962), it was to remain a branch of the Adamant Co-op.

Decades of Retrenchment -- and a Couple of Near-death Experiences

By the war years, the Co-op's founders had every right to feel they had figured out the best way to organize the economic life of their community. Each of the organizations they had created -- the Adamant Co-op, its Maple Corner branch, the Washington Electric Cooperative, and the Adamant Credit Union -- was an authentic expression of the people who staffed, sustained, and were served by

them. Together these organizations promoted a generous, enlightened attitude toward social issues that enriched the life of their communities. There was no reason to doubt that they would be able to fulfill their mission indefinitely.

But from the 1950s on, the impetus faltered. The broader economy grew more prosperous, which undercut the basis for the early success of Adamant's cooperative movement.

A general increase in wealth, plus better, more affordable transportation made it easier for people to get out and for goods to get in. Self-contained villages metamorphosed into bedroom communities from which residents commuted to their jobs elsewhere. Low-cost producers in the Midwest and beyond became able to ship their goods long distances and to displace local providers saddled with higher costs of production. The era of the shopping center dawned.

In 1973, an untimely end was averted at the eleventh hour when shareholders overturned a board vote to terminate the Co-op. They kept it in operation and voted instead to sell off the Maple Corner Store.

In 1986, the Adamant Credit Union was, in its turn, dissolved and its assets absorbed into a larger credit union.

By February 1990, the New York Times was announcing the Co-op's impending demise: "Short of a miracle, the Adamant Co-op is likely to go out of business this spring. But a miracle of sorts has already happened. After the nine-member co-op board voted in December to close the store on Jan. 31, fifteen neighbors promised to donate a total of $450 a month through April to keep the store running."

To save its Co-op, Adamant replayed its founding act.

A Quiet Renaissance

And so it has run ever since.

The Adamant Co-op has since arisen with rosy cheek and bouncing step from a long, seemingly terminal decline. An aura of the miraculous does seem to pervade it, a sense of some transcendent Adamant without borders, pulsing with a common heart while relating to people's everyday lives in the most down-to-earth way.

Beyond the mystique, a number of hard facts

help to keep Adamant and its co-op alive. Despite the T-shirt's bravado, "All roads lead to Adamant," geography concentrates people into a discrete space that is just isolated enough to give it an individual character, but not so isolated as to make it a stagnant backwater. By straddling the boundary between Calais and East Montpelier, Adamant assures itself a primary identity of its own. Enough farming and market gardening are still going on in the area to satisfy people's reawakened appreciation for the fruits of local soil and toil.

At the same time, the Co-op is a secular offspring of the Adamant United Methodist Church and a close neighbor of the Adamant Music School, two other local institutions where the community soul burns bright. The power of this commercial-spiritual-cultural nexus to animate the lives of its residents can be experienced -- and in some cases, purchased outright -- in the arts, crafts, food, music, writing, film making, theater, and naturalist pursuits of "Greater Adamant."

So, harking back to Janet MacLeod's observation: Adamant people want to buy the things their friends and neighbors make. They want to cross paths with their neighbors, to commune around the wood stove, to work together on festivals and cook-outs, and the little tasks of maintaining and helping hold the whole shoestring enterprise together.

And having had the chance to sample each other's cooking over the years, Adamant people have long since discovered that they love each other's food. This cookbook is both a gift and a token of gratitude drawn from our history. Tradition, creativity, beauty, and the sheer joy of life--the spirit of Adamant--all come together in these pages, not unlike the ingredients in the recipes you find within them.

My mother was once denied a request for a recipe she had made of an acquaintance with the response: "I am not promiscuous with my recipes." This cookbook wouldn't have been possible without the generous contributions of their most favored recipes by the good cooks of Adamant.

Promiscuous? I call it Sharing.   --Barbara Weedon

A VISIT WITH FRIENDS
by Barbara Weedon

I have a box of recipes that are companions in my kitchen. They are written on a motley assortment of papers. Some are written in pencil, others in various shades of ink, and a very few are neatly typed on index cards. They are brown with age and use, splattered and be-smudged, with torn edges, dog-eared and fading. I look for a recipe, and at the sight of familiar handwriting I am warmed.

RED AND GREEN PEPPER RELISH with Marilyn. We pushed baby buggies together as young brides and made this relish in my kitchen while our five children under six years of age hung onto our apron strings. How did we manage to do that?

SAND TARTS. Helen's Christmas cookie. I could never manage to roll them as thinly as she did. She was a mother-in-law who was lavish with praise and encouragement, who never spoke a word of criticism or control. Her hot, flakey breakfast biscuits are unforgettable and impossible to replicate.

THE BEST THANKSGIVING TURKEY STUFFING from Yvonne, a college roommate. It WAS the best, and has been part of our traditional holiday menu for fifty years.

ZUPPA di PASTA e FAGIOLI, from Laura, best friend and best cook. Laura was an Italian war bride. Hugh introduced her to his army buddy when they were stationed in Italy in World War II. Laura's generosity is reflected in her recipes. Never stingy, she instructs, "add a good fistful of . . .".

TRADITIONAL CZECH DISHES written out for me in lovely Palmer Penmanship by my mother. These are the dishes I grew up eating, and though some have not been favored by my family, they help to anchor me to my past. I feel an obligation to preserve them.

EDIE'S ZUCCHINI BREAD. My cousin Edie never arrived for a visit without a cake in hand. She baked for all occasions, to celebrate, to console, to greet a new neighbor, to take to a friend whose husband had left her--that one went down in family lore as the Divorce Cake.

And on it goes . . . times past, memories, good food . . . all brought to mind as I search through this little box--a visit with old and dear friends.

Breakfast at
the Co-op

As I walk up the Co-op steps, two geese are honking their way into the mist that has settled over Sodom Pond. The air is cool and fresh.

I turn on lights, move wine bottles forward, replace yesterday's newspaper with today's. My son Cameron sets out the "Open" flag and helps with sorting the mail. We have a routine -- he does the post boxes on the right-hand side and I do the left.

The first customer picks up milk, eggs, salad, and a bottle of wine. A good start to the day. The school bus stops and inhales the small gaggle of kids outside, including Cameron. It's quiet now. The only noise comes from the cooler compressor. I finish sorting the mail. Manghi's Bread calls to see if we need an order. Bruce comes in to check his mail. A stranger stops in to ask for directions and buys a couple of doughnuts for the road. Pat arrives with a plate of still-warm blueberry muffins. They go between the scones and the brownies.

A young woman comes in. She's visiting a friend here and loves the Co-op. She looks down at her pajamas and smiles sheepishly. "I just need coffee; my friend had to run into Montpelier." She picks our strongest, and while it's brewing, begins nibbling at a muffin.

She pays for coffee and two muffins and calls out as she leaves, "This place is great -- where else can you buy coffee in your pajamas?"

--Regina Thompson

BLUEBERRY MUFFINS

1 stick butter, at room temperature
1 cup granulated sugar
2 eggs
1 teaspoon vanilla extract
2 teaspoons baking powder
A pinch of salt
2 ½ cups blueberries (mash ½ cup with a fork)
2 cups all purpose flour
½ cup milk

Pre-heat the oven to 375 degrees F.
Grease the muffin tin.
In a large bowl, beat the butter until creamy, add the sugar and beat until pale.
Beat in one egg at a time.
Beat in the vanilla, baking powder, and salt.
Add the mashed berries, mix.
Fold in half the flour, then half the milk, then the remaining flour.
Fold in the remaining blueberries.
Divide the batter into muffin tin. Bake 25 - 30 minutes.
Let cool -- enjoy.
Yields 12

ADAMANT MAPLE WALNUT MUFFINS

Makes 12 muffins.

Preheat oven to 375 degrees F. Spray medium-sized
muffin tins with Pam.
Mix together:
1 ¼ cups flour
½ teaspoon salt
1 teaspoon baking powder
½ cup brown sugar
1 cup chopped walnuts
Mix together:
1 cup sour cream
5 teaspoons softened butter
2 slightly beaten eggs
½ cup maple syrup

Add the wet ingredients to the dry ingredients and mix
gently. Spoon into muffin pan.
Top each muffin with one half of a walnut.
Bake 20 – 25 minutes, until a toothpick comes out
clean. Let rest 10 minutes and then
remove from pan.

TOO MANY ZUCCHINIS BREAD

Vermont's growing season is very short. One of the things that grow fantastically well are zucchinis. In late August and early September you will often see a pile of them on somebody's front lawn with a big "FREE" sign next to them. Also, it is advisable to lock your car during zucchini season--not so much because we are worried about burglars but somebody just might sneak a whole bunch of zucchinis into your car.....

Ingredients:
1 ½ cups zucchini, shredded
¾ cup sugar
2 eggs
½ cup vegetable oil
1 ½ cups flour
½ teaspoon each baking soda and baking powder
A pinch of salt
1 teaspoon cinnamon
The zest of one lemon
2 teaspoons lemon juice

Preheat the oven to 350 degrees F and grease a 5 ¾ x 9 ¾ x 2 ¾ inch loaf pan.

Beat together sugar, eggs, oil, and zucchini. Sift in the flour, baking powder and soda, and salt. Add the cinnamon, lemon, and lemon zest. Stir until the mixture is blended (do not overmix). Pour batter into prepared pan. Bake for 45 minutes (until knife comes out clean). Let cool.

BREAKFAST EMPANADAS

Use recipe for empanada dough on page 67.
Preheat the oven to 375 degrees F.

9 large eggs plus one more beaten with 1 tablespoon of water for egg wash
About 8 ounces very sharp cheddar
12 slices crisp cooked bacon chopped into large pieces
Your favorite salsa
Olive oil

Scramble the eggs, but stop cooking when they are still a bit wet. They are going to cook more in the oven.
On each empanada shell place some eggs, bacon, cheese, and salsa ONLY on one half of the dough. Make sure to leave a clean border of about ½ inch so the edges of the empanada will stick together.
With a pastry brush, brush egg wash around the edge, fold over top, and use a fork to crimp the edges together. If some filling begins to sneak out, don't be afraid to use your fingers to push it back in. You'll have to find out how much filling you can use.
Put the filled empanada on a baking sheet lined with parchment paper.
When all of the empanadas are filled, brush all of the tops with the remaining egg wash.
Bake until the dough becomes a light golden brown and the edges a darker brown.
Yields 12 empanadas.

LEMON BLUEBERRY MUFFINS WITH STREUSEL TOPPING

Preheat the oven to 400 degrees F. Grease muffin pan.
Makes 12 large muffins—best to use large sized muffin pan –
usually 6 muffins to a pan, so you will need two pans).
Ingredients:
4 cups flour
1 cup sugar
4 teaspoons baking powder
1 teaspoon baking soda
1 teaspoon salt
4 eggs, lightly beaten
16 ounces lemon yogurt
1 cup vegetable oil
2 cups blueberries
Streusel Topping:
1/3 cup sugar
¼ cup flour
2 tablespoons. butter

In a large bowl, combine the first five
ingredients. Combine eggs, yogurt, and
oil in another large bowl, mixing well.
Stir dried ingredients gently into wet
ingredients. Fold in blueberries. Fill muffin
pans ¾ full. For streusel, combine sugar and
flour. Cut in butter until mixture is like course
crumbs.Sprinkle about 1 tablespoon on each muffin.
Bake 18 – 20 minutes or until a toothpick comes out
clean.Cool in pan 10 minutes, and then remove to wire
rack.

SPICED PUMPKIN MUFFINS

1 stick butter at room temperature
3/4 cup brown sugar
1/3 cup molasses
1 egg (beaten) at room temperature
1 cup cooked pumpkin
1 3/4 cups flour
A pinch of salt
1 teaspoon baking soda
2 teaspoons ground cinnamon
1 teaspoon nutmeg
1/4 cup raisins

Preheat the oven to 400 degrees F and grease muffin tin.
Cream butter.
Add sugar and molasses -- beat a couple of minutes.
Add egg and pumpkin -- stir until well blended.
Add sifted flour, salt, baking soda, cinnamon, and nutmeg
-- blend just enough.
Fold in raisins.
Spoon batter into greased muffin tins,
Bake until tops spring back when touched lightly (around 15 minutes).
Yields 12 muffins.

CRANBERRY BREAD

2 cups flour
1/2 cup sugar
1 tablespoon baking powder
1/2 teaspoon salt
Grated rind of one orange
2/3 cup orange juice
2 eggs (beaten) at room temperature
6 tablespoons butter
1 1/4 cups fresh cranberries
1/2 cup chopped walnuts

Preheat oven to 350 degrees F. Grease pan.
Sift flour, sugar, baking powder, and salt into bowl
Stir in orange rind.
Add orange juice, eggs, and melted butter -- stir until well blended.
Add cranberries and walnuts -- blend.
Pour batter into baking pan -- bake for about 50 minutes.

CRANBERRY AND CHOCOLATE CHIP MUFFINS

1 cup sugar
½ stick of butter (softened)
2 eggs
1 cup whole wheat flour
1 ½ cups white flour
2 teaspoon baking powder
½ cup milk
2 cups fresh or frozen cranberries
12 ounces semi-sweet chocolate chips

Preheat the oven to 400 degrees F and grease a large
12-muffin baking pan.
In a large bowl, cream together sugar and butter. Add eggs
and beat thoroughly. Add flours and baking powder. Add
milk. Divide batter into approximate halves in the bowl.
Add and mix cranberries to one half. Spoon into one half of
the muffin pan--approximately ¾ full. Add and mix the
chocolate chips to the other half of batter. Spoon into
other half of the muffin pan. Bake for 16-20 minutes.

Makes six cranberry muffins and six chocolate chip muffins.
(Smaller, but more muffins if you use a smaller muffin
pan!) If you prefer just cranberry muffins, add an additional
2 cups of cranberries and omit the chocolate chips. Low fat
version: Use 1/8 cup (2 tablespoons) butter and 1/8 cup (2
tablespoons) apple sauce for the ½ stick of butter. (May
need to reduce the milk slightly.)

STICKY BUNS

For many years BethAnn Porter was an event at the Adamant Co-op. As the primary chef de cuisine for breakfast and lunch treats, she would whirl through the front door of the Co-op, trays in hand, vibrant clothing and personality matched only by the addictiveness of her food--sticky buns, southern style ribs, chocolate ganache cake. We asked BethAnn for recipes, but as it is with most great artists, her recipes exist only in the moment: a pinch of this, a dollop of that, mixed with the inspiration of the season, weather, or mood. What about the sticky buns we asked? "Just take any sticky bun recipe and double the butter and frosting," she replied. Here is a substitute recipe for BethAnn's sticky buns. Double the butter and frosting at your own risk!
Makes 9 buns

For the Dough

2/3 cup whole milk
5 tablespoons sugar, in all
1 3/4 teaspoons active dry yeast (one envelope)
2 large eggs, room temperature
2 3/4 cups unbleached all-purpose flour
1 teaspoon kosher salt
1/2 cup (1 stick) unsalted butter, cut into 1-inch pieces, at room temperature, plus 1/2 tablespoon, melted

Preparation:

Heat milk in a small saucepan over medium heat or in a microwave to 110–115 degrees F. Transfer milk to a 2-cup measuring cup or bowl and stir in 1 tablespoon sugar. Sprinkle yeast over milk and whisk to blend. Let sit until yeast is foamy, about 5 minutes. Add eggs and whisk until smooth.

Combine remaining 4 tablespoons sugar, flour, and salt in the bowl of a stand mixer fitted with a dough hook. Add milk mixture. With mixer running, add 1/2 cup of the room-temperature butter, 1 piece at a time, blending well between additions. Mix on medium speed for 1 minute. Knead on medium-high speed until dough is soft and silky, about 5 minutes.

(Note: If you don't have a stand mixer, fit your food processor with the dough blade. Combine the 4 tablespoons sugar, the flour, and the salt in food processor bowl. Pulse to blend. Add milk mixture; process until combined. With processor running, add 1/2 cup room-temperature butter, 1 piece at a time, blending well between additions. Process until dough is soft and silky, 2–3 minutes longer. Dough will be sticky but should not be greasy. If it is greasy, process for an additional 1–2 minutes.)

Melt the remaining tablespoon of butter and brush a medium bowl with it; Place dough in bowl. Brush top of dough with remaining melted butter; cover with plastic wrap. (Note: Can be made one day ahead. Cover with plastic; chill.)

Let dough rise in a warm, draft-free area until doubled in

size, 1 to 1 ½ hours (or 2 to 2 ½ hours if the dough has been refrigerated overnight). Chill risen dough for 2 hours.

For the Topping:

1 ¾ cups pecans (about 8 ounces), coarsely chopped
½ cup (1 stick) unsalted butter
¾ cup (packed) dark brown sugar
¾ cup heavy cream
1/3 cup honey
¼ teaspoon kosher salt

Preparation:
Preheat oven to 350 degrees F. Spread nuts on a rimmed baking sheet. Toast until fragrant and slightly darkened, 10-12 minutes. Let cool completely. Set 1 ¼ cups nuts aside for buns.

Melt butter in a small heavy saucepan over medium heat. Stir in brown sugar, cream, honey, and salt. Bring to a boil, reduce heat to medium, and simmer until glaze is golden brown and glossy, 3-4 minutes. Pour 1 cup of glaze into baking pan, tilting to coat bottom and sides. Set aside remaining glaze. Sprinkle ½ cup toasted pecans over bottom of baking pan and let cool.

For the Buns:

½ cup (1 stick) unsalted butter at room temperature
½ cup (packed) dark brown sugar
¾ teaspoon ground cinnamon
½ teaspoon freshly grated nutmeg
1/8 teaspoon kosher salt

All-purpose flour (for dusting)
1 large egg
Coarse sea salt (such as Maldon)

Special equipment: An 8 x 8 x 2-inch metal baking pan

Preparation:
Using an electric mixer on medium speed, beat butter, sugar, cinnamon, nutmeg, and kosher salt in a medium bowl until light and fluffy, 2-3 minutes. Set filling aside.

Punch down dough; transfer to a floured work surface. Lightly dust top with flour.

Roll out the dough into a 12 x 16-inch rectangle about ¼-inch thick. Arrange the dough on the work surface so one long side faces you. Spread the cinnamon-sugar mixture over dough, leaving a 1-inch plain border on the side farthest from you.

Sprinkle ¾ cup chopped pecans over the cinnamon-sugar mixture. Beginning with the long edge closest to you, roll dough into a log, tightening as you roll, and patting in ends if they begin to taper. Pinch together the seam where the long side meets the roll to seal. Arrange the log seam-side down on the work surface.

Using a large knife, cut the log crosswise into 9 equal pieces. Lightly flour the knife between slices if the dough is too sticky. Turn the buns cut side up and gently pat the top to flatten slightly. If needed, reshape to form round edges by cupping lightly floured hands around each bun and gently pushing and turning them in a circular motion. Place the buns in prepared pan; space them evenly apart (buns should not touch each other).

(Note: Can be made one day ahead. Cover and chill buns and remaining glaze separately. Store remaining pecans in an airtight container at room temperature.)

Loosely cover pan with plastic wrap or a kitchen towel. Let buns rise in a warm, draft-free area until doubled in size, 45 minutes to 1 hour, or 1 ½ to 2 hours if the formed buns have been chilled overnight.

Arrange a rack in middle of oven; preheat to 350 F. Whisk egg with ½ teaspoon water in a small bowl. Brush tops of buns with egg wash. Bake, rotating pan halfway through (after about 25 minutes). Tent with foil if the buns brown too quickly, Continue baking until the buns are golden brown, the filling is bubbling, and an instant-read thermometer inserted into center of buns registers 185 degrees F, about 50 minutes in total. Let cool for 5 minutes. Spoon remaining glaze over buns. Sprinkle the ½ cup of remaining pecans over the buns. Let cool in pan on a wire rack.

Lightly sprinkle sea salt over the buns. Serve buns warm or at room temperature.

GRANOLA

The original recipe came from Adele Davis, who was the nutritional guru for the parents of those of us who grew up in the 1950s. I'm not even sure how much I've changed it.

5 cups of regular rolled oats
1 cup each powdered milk, soy flour, wheat germ
1 cup nuts (slivered almonds, peanuts, or cashews)
1 cup sunflower seeds
(optional) 1 cup sesame seed. I leave them out because they so often end up on the bottom of the granola jar.
3/4 plus 1 cup oil. I like peanut or canola.
1/2 to 3/4 cup honey or agave

Mix all the dry ingredients together, then add oil followed by sweetener. If you measure the oil first, when you measure out the sweetener, it slides out of the cup easily.

Bake on cookie sheets in very low oven until it's golden brown. Half-way through baking stir the granola to bring the lighter grains to the top.

Soup's On

Linda sorts through the boxes of produce that just arrived. "Of course it's in the last one", she mutters as she pulls out a beautiful butternut squash. "Like any lost item found, it's always in the last place you look," I quip.

Later, mouth-watering aromas begin to waft down from the kitchen. My stomach tells me it's time for lunch. Soon Linda comes down with a steaming pot of butternut squash soup. "Soup's on," she tells Janet.

Whether it's freshly made in the Co-op kitchen or a frozen block of chowder from Screaming Ridge Farm placed into a stock pot on the wood stove to thaw and reheat, nothing chases the chill with friendly warmth like soup at the Co-op.

--Regina Thompson

BUTTERNUT SQUASH SOUP WITH GINGER

500 grams (1 pound) butternut squash
1 onion
1 potato
1 walnut size piece of ginger
1 can of coconut milk (400 grams/14 ounces)
2 teaspoons of red curry paste (or 2 tablespoons curry powder)
400 milliliters (14 ounces) vegetable broth

Peel the squash and cut into small pieces. Finely cut the onion. Peel the potato and cut into small pieces. Peel and cut the ginger.

Open the coconut milk and put the thick cream into a pot; heat slowly. Add onion, ginger, and curry; stir and let cook for about 5 minutes. Add squash; cook for about 2 minutes. Add remaining coconut milk, broth, potato, and salt. Cook until vegetables are soft (about 20 minutes). Puree and season to taste.

Guests coming over? Garnish soup with roasted pumpkin seeds or a few dribbles of pumpkin seed oil.

Wine pairing; Enjoy this soup with a good dry Riesling. Butternut squash has a rich, nutty taste and is a "must have" ingredient in the autumn and winter kitchen. This

hearty and soul warming soup is not only a great winter favorite but also very popular during the holiday season. Imagine, coming home after a long snowshoe hike in the woods to the mouth watering smells of squash and ginger.

VOLHYNIAN BEET SOUP (Barszcz Wolynski)

We have heard that this soup is referred to as "rotten apple soup" in Richard Czaplinski's family. The story as we know it is that Richard was making the soup one day and his daughter noticed a rotten apple sitting on the counter near the ingredients for the soup. Later the apple and the soup's ingredients were gone, and she made the assumption the apple went into the soup. She never ate the soup again. Recipe taken from Treasured Polish Recipes for Americans, Polanie Club, Marie Sokolowski and Irene Jasinski, editors, Minneapolis, Minnesota. 1948. Somewhat modified by Richard Czaplinski. Oh, and no rotten apple required.

6 medium beets
1 head of cabbage (I use a lot less)
4 large tomatoes [I use a jar of tomato juice or sauce)
Meat stock (I make a vegetable stock by sautéing (in oil or butter) onions, carrots, garlic, peppers, leeks celery, parsley, and basil, or whatever vegetables you may have on hand]
1 sour apple (or even a sweet one)
¼ cup of beans (soaked overnight)
Sour rye bread crust (I don't add this, if you do, it is taken out before serving)
Salt and pepper

Start the night before by soaking the beans. Have the beans simmering in the soaking pot while you sauté the vegetables. Sauté the vegetables in a good sized pot. Add salt and pepper and dry basil (or use fresh basil in the sautéing). Add the tomato juice or sauce. Peel and cube the beets into bite-sized pieces and add to the pot. Slice up the cabbage into bite size or a bit larger pieces and add to the pot. When things are simmering in the pot, drain the cooking water from the beans and add them to the pot. Cut up the apple and add to the pot. Simmer for an hour or two until beets and beans are tender.

Serve hot with a spoonful of sour cream. Very good with a slice of fresh bread and butter.

ANDREA'S END OF SUMMER -- WHATEVER-IS-IN-THE-GARDEN SOUP

2-3 tablespoons butter
Leeks and/or onions (as much as you want)
1 or 2 carrots
2 or 3 potatoes (depending on size)
1 quart or more chicken or vegetable stock, warmed
3 tablespoons flour
Fresh parsley and dill
And whatever's in the garden: corn, green beans, peas, zucchini-- whatever you think is fitting
Salt and pepper to taste
Diced leftover chicken if you want

Sauté onions and leeks and carrots slowly in butter until soft and transparent. Stir in the flour until thoroughly mixed, then add the warmed stock slowly, whisking as you do. Bring it all to a simmer, Cover and let simmer until the potatoes are close to done.

Add the other vegetables and the herbs, simmer until just tender. Salt and pepper to taste. Add chicken at the very end. This soup tastes best if you let it sit for an hour or so, then gently reheat.

This soup is wonderfully receptive to variation. Have fun with it!

REBECCA'S FAVORITE GAZPACHO

1 cucumber, grated
1 green pepper, finely chopped
1 kilogram (about 2 ¼ pounds) ripe tomatoes, chopped
1 onion, chopped
5 garlic cloves, crushed
5 tablespoons olive oil
4 tablespoons white wine vinegar
2 tablespoons lemon or lime juice
1 liter (4 cups) tomato juice
salt and pepper to taste

Blend the tomatoes, onion and garlic.
Add olive oil, vinegar, lemon or lime juice. Blend until smooth.
Add grated cucumber and chopped green pepper. Add tomato juice.
Season to taste and chill (at least 6 hours).

PORTUGUESE-STYLE EAT-MORE-KALE SOUP
(Serves about 4)

About 2 tablespoons extra virgin olive oil
1 large or 2 medium onions, chopped
1 clove garlic, minced
About 1 pound fresh kale, de-ribbed, washed, and coarsely chopped
1 to 1 ½ quarts beef stock
1-2 teaspoons Spanish paprika or to taste
About 2-3 cups peeled, seeded, and chopped fresh tomatoes or one 15-ounce can tomatoes crushed by hand
12 to 16 ounces Portuguese-style chorico or linguica sausage (for example, Gaspar's brand)

Heat olive oil in a large soup pot. Add onions and garlic and cook slowly until softened (not browned), about 5 minutes. Add kale, cover and cook, stirring, until wilted. Add stock, paprika, and tomatoes and bring to a simmer. Cut sausage into small rounds (linguica) or half moons (chorico) and add to soup. Return to simmer and cook about 10 minutes. Check seasoning and add salt and pepper if desired. Serve with warm, crusty French or country bread.

(Options: To make it spicier, add a pinch of red pepper flakes to the onions and garlic while they cook. To make the soup heartier, peel and dice about three medium Yukon gold potatoes and cook them along with the onions and garlic for five minutes. Another variation is to add one 15-oz can of drained and rinsed cannellini beans along with the stock and tomatoes)

CREAM OF CHICKEN SOUP

Yield: About 8 servings

¼ cup butter
¼ cup olive oil
1 large yellow onion, diced
2 stalks celery, diced
3 large carrots, chopped
½ cup flour
7 cups chicken stock (store-bought is fine)
2 bay leaves
2 tablespoons or more dried tarragon
1-2 tablespoons granulated garlic
3-4 cups cooked, diced chicken breast
½ cup heavy cream
3-5 tablespoons golden sherry (or any other kind you have. Start with smaller amount and add more if desired)
Salt and pepper to taste

Melt butter and olive oil in large pot over medium heat. Add vegetables and cook, covered, until they are just soft. They won't cook much more after this, so get them as done as you like. They shouldn't be overly soft. Add flour and continue cooking, stirring constantly, for a couple of minutes to take the raw taste out of the flour. Don't let it burn.
Stream in stock gradually whisking at first to keep it smooth and then switching to a wooden spoon. Bring to a boil and add tarragon, garlic, and bay leaves. Turn to low, and simmer for about 10 minutes. Stir in

chicken and bring to a boil. Remove from heat: add sherry, cream, salt and pepper. Adjust seasonings. You may need more sherry, garlic, etc.

Lunch, Dinner, and Other Good Stuff

The Kitchens of Adamant

The Co-op kitchen gives us breakfast and lunch, burgers and dogs and pizza. It's our gathering spot where we grab food and companionship. But it's the kitchens in our homes where the food that truly binds us is made. In our kitchens, we cook up condolences in our losses, nourishment in our illnesses, celebration when we'd otherwise be alone. We lend a hand when our neighbors need it. We dice, chop, and bake ourselves through our hard times and our joy. Adamant is a diverse community full of independent-minded people, but no matter the opinions or politics, we all feel obliged to help each other out. Maybe that's one definition of community.

--Barbara Floersch

QUICHE WITH RAMPS (WILD LEEKS)

This is a nice way to use spring ramps or wild leeks (similar to wild garlic), but feel free to use six to eight sliced green onions and a clove or two of minced garlic. Bacon, cheese, tomatoes, and mushrooms help make this quiche hearty and extra-flavorful.

Prepare your favorite pie crust

6 - 8 slices bacon, diced
8 ounces mushrooms chopped
2 cups chopped ramps
1 cup diced tomatoes
1/2 teaspoon ground black pepper
3 eggs
1 cup half-and-half
4-6 ounces Cheddar cheese
A pinch of ground nutmeg

Pre-heat the oven to 375 degrees F. Prepare pie crust. Cook bacon until crisp; drain on paper towels. Pour off all but about 2 tablespoons of the bacon drippings. Add the mushrooms and ramps to the skillet and cook, stirring, until mushrooms are tender. Add the tomatoes, salt, and pepper. Cook for about 1 minute longer. Spoon the cooked vegetables into the crust; top with the cheese.

In a bowl, whisk together the eggs, half-and-half, and nutmeg. Pour the egg mixture over the cheese layer and gently use a spoon to help the egg mixture sink into the vegetables.
Set the pie on a foil-lined baking sheet and bake for 35 to 45 minutes, or until set and lightly browned. A knife inserted into the center should come out clean.

Serves 6 to 8.

In winter, all life is drawn to the kitchen. Gourmands of warmth, cats lie so close to the woodstove it's a wonder they don't combust. It is an odd combination of textures and shapes, hot, angular cast iron and porcelain, a soft mound of warm fur curled close by, but both are beating hearts in a winter kitchen, keeping icy stillness at bay beyond frosted panes.

ENCHILADAS

2 cups (8 ounces) shredded Monterey Jack cheese
2 cups (10 ounces) shredded cooked chicken
1/3 cup chopped tomatoes
1/3 cup chopped black olives
1/3 cup canned chopped green chili peppers
1/3 cup chopped onions
4 cups salsa
10 flour or corn tortillas

Preheat oven to 350 degrees F. Grease 3-quart rectangular baking dish.

In a bowl stir together 1 cup cheese, the chicken, tomatoes, olives, chili peppers, onions and 1 cup salsa -- mix. Place remaining salsa in shallow dish. Dip tortillas in the salsa, one at a time. Spoon about 1/3 cup of chicken mixture into center of each tortilla. Roll up and place into baking dish, seam side down. Pour remaining salsa over tortillas. Cover with foil and put in oven for 30 minutes. Remove foil. Sprinkle with remaining cheese and return to oven for about 5 minutes.

POT ROAST, THE "DOUG SPECIAL"

Until his sudden death, Doug Nicholson delivered the mail to the Adamant Post Office. Doug was always helpful, especially when it came to guiding us through arcane USPS regulations. He was also quick to join in rough-and-tumble banter or to take the opposite side of an argument, regardless of the topic. Doug was truly a carnivore, He loved things like Ball Park Franks, but this pot roast was one of his favorites.

2 tablespoons bacon grease
4 pounds pot roast (chuck roast)
2 cloves garlic cut in thirds
2 onions chopped
2 cups chopped carrots
2 cups chopped parsnips
2 cups beef stock
2 cups red wine
2 bay leaves
1 teaspoon thyme
6 - 8 potatoes, halved
Salt and pepper

Preheat the oven to 325 degrees F.

Make deep incisions in the meat and insert garlic pieces. Heat bacon grease and brown roast on all sides. Remove and set aside. Add onions, carrots, and parsnips. Cook over low heat until softened.

Add stock, wine, and herbs. Return roast to pan, cover, and place in preheated oven for 1 hour, 30 minutes. Add potatoes, season with salt and pepper, cover, and return to oven for another hour.

In a small bowl combine flour and some water--make a paste. Transfer meat and all vegetables to a serving platter. Discard bay leaves. Bring cooking liquid to a boil--add flour paste and whisk until thickened. Serve with the roast.

Wine: enjoy with a glass of Merlot -- or in Doug's case, buy a bottle of wine with a crazy name or funky label for your wine collection and enjoy the roast with a pint of milk.

LENTIL QUICHE

For the dough:
150 grams (about ½ cup) flour
150 grams (about ½ cup) ricotta cheese
150 grams (about 10 tablespoons) cold butter - cut into pieces
2 teaspoons curry powder
salt

For the filling:
1 - 2 onions, chopped
2 tablespoons olive oil
2 garlic cloves, crushed
fresh ginger (about the size of a walnut)- cut into very small pieces
250 grams (about ½ pound) red lentils
salt and pepper
2 teaspoons curry powder
500 milliliters (about 2 cups) vegetable broth
2 tomatoes
50 milliliters (3 tablespoons) milk
1 egg

Put flour, ricotta, cold butter, salt, and curry into a bowl and make a dough. Let rest for 30 minutes. Thinly slice onion and saute. Add garlic and ginger. Continue to saute for about 3 minutes.
Add lentils, salt, pepper, curry powder, and vegetable broth. Bring to boil, cover, and simmer for about 15 minutes. Let cool down a bit. Mix together milk and eggs. Cut tomatoes into small pieces. Preheat oven to about 400 degrees F (200 degrees C).

Grease pie dish and put dough in dish. Mix tomatoes into lentil mixture. Pour lentil mixture on top of dough. Add milk and egg mixture.

Bake for about 35 minutes.

BOEUF ADAMANT

1 onion, chopped
1 ½ pounds chuck steak, cubed
1 teaspoon thyme
1 tablespoon parsley
500 milliliters (about 2 cups) red wine
60 milliliters (4 tablespoons) brandy
2 tablespoons olive oil

50 grams (3 tablespoons) butter
6 rashers (slices) bacon, chopped
12 peeled pickling onions
250 grams (½ pound) Crimini mushrooms, quartered
2 tablespoons all-purpose flour
400 milliliters (about 2 cups) beef stock

Put onion, steak, herbs, wine and brandy in a bowl, cover and marinate for at least 3 hours.
Heat 1 tablespoon olive oil and 25 grams (1 ½ tablespoons) butter in large heavy-based pot. Cook bacon and pickling onions on low heat until onions are golden brown. Remove onions and bacon. Set aside.
Add mushrooms and cook for 3 - 4 minutes. Remove and set aside.
Add remaining oil and butter. Brown meat in batches. Return all meat to pot and sprinkle with flour until well coated. Add marinade and beef stock. Bring to boil, cover, and simmer on low heat until meat is very tender (1 to 1 ½ hours).
Add pickling onions, bacon, and mushrooms. Cook uncovered for 15 minutes.
Season to taste.

Serve with mashed potatoes or egg noodles.

CHEESE AND SPINACH TART

½ cup plus 1 tablespoon fine bread crumbs
1/3 cup grated parmesan cheese
2 tablespoons melted butter
2 tablespoons sour cream
1 pound cottage cheese
2 tablespoons flour
2 eggs
1 box of frozen chopped spinach, cooked and well drained
¼ pound diced ham

Mix ½ cup of bread crumbs with 2 tablespoons parmesan cheese and 2 tablespoons melted butter and press into a 9-inch pie pan to make a crust (unbaked).

Beat remaining parmesan cheese, 2 tablespoons sour cream, 2 tablespoons flour, 2 eggs, and 1 pound cottage cheese. Then mix HALF of it with the spinach and HALF of it with the diced ham. Spread the spinach mixture in the pie pan. Top it with the ham mixture and sprinkle the top with 1 tablepsoon bread crumbs.

Bake for 40 minutes (or until set) at 350 degrees F.

Serve with dollops of sour cream at a table set under your favorite shade tree along with a plate of summer-ripe sliced tomatoes and basil. A cold crisp white wine, or iced tea, wouldnt go amiss. The pie is good hot as well as a cold picnic item.

FRITTATA (quiche without a crust)

2 tablespoons olive oil
12 large eggs
4 cups heavy cream
1 cup grated parmigiano-reggiano cheese
2 cups chopped bacon, or ham, or turkey bacon, or
sausage, or if you want to keep it vegetarian, then something like roasted red peppers, sun dried tomatoes, something with a bit of saltiness or a kick
1 large onion, sliced thin
A good amount of fresh spinach
Any vegetables you have in the fridge that you like and
think would be good in this
Fresh dill, chopped fine
Salt, pepper
8 ounces very sharp cheddar sliced thin, or your favorite
melting cheese

In a large bowl beat the eggs, then beat in the cream, the
parmesgiano-reggiano, salt, pepper and dill (or any other
herbs you'd like to use). Set aside.

Heat the olive oil in a large, non-stick pan. Saute the
onions until soft. If your other veggies need to be cooked
(mushrooms, peppers, whatever), add them along with the
onions. Also add meat if using.

When the veggies are done (they shouldn't be mushy, you
want to keep things pretty fresh), add the fresh spinach and
cook briefly, stirring, until the spinach has wilted. It's
amazing how much spinach cooks down. Turn the heat up
to high for a minute. Then pour in the egg mixture and

immediately turn the heat down to the lowest setting.
Cook on top of the stove until it seems like the eggs are
cooked about halfway through. Some bubbles will begin
to appear on the top. Use a spatula to keep pulling in the
cooked edges, tilting the pan to allow the liquid part to
spread out the the edges. It can take 5-10 minutes to get
to the right stage.

Put the sliced cheddar all over the top of the eggs.

Turn the oven to broil. Place the pan in the oven, about
8-10 inches from the flame. I wrap the handle in foil to
keep it from getting damaged in the oven. Cook under the
broiler until the eggs are completely set and the top is
beautifully brown. You'll have to jiggle the pan and maybe
stick a knife into it to make sure the eggs are done. If it
begins to get too brown on top before getting done, turn
the broiler off and bake at 350 degrees F until done.

CHANTERELLES
By Barbara Floersch

The first year we found the chanterelles they were prolific, a riot of orange-gold parasols poking up through decaying hemlock needles into the filtered sunlight. We had walked far down the old farm road, then turned onto a trail through the town forest. The summer was deep and heavy and nearly gone. Wild roses had hardened into smooth green hips and goldenrod waved in the tall grass. In summer the old farm road is a long green canyon only occasionally lit by blue sky. It's warm there and filled with buzzing things. There's a feeling of industriousness about it; nature getting on with things and oblivious to humans.

We hadn't been on a mission or a pilgrimage. We hadn't expected to find anything except perhaps some of the suspended time a forest walk can bring. Then there they were, where the trail levels out and the land flattens into a swampy place that was once a beaver pond—a landscape of creamy gold mushrooms emerging from composted needles, hugging close to the moss by the hemlocks, sprinkled helter-skelter. The breath we exhaled said "Ooooo," and then we laughed.

It's a serious matter to pick a chanterelle. Plucking nature's gold comes with mighty responsibilities. They are so tender to the touch, so easily bruised. They are damp and slightly sticky. They smell of the rich, dank earth. Even the daintiest fingers thicken and fumble in trying so hard to be gentle.

The cathedral of the chanterelles laid itself before us and offered a promise and a burden. The tender sweetness of the earth is yours: savor it. This moment of the chanterelles is now and may not come again. Pluck the gift reverently and also with joy. We were quiet then, each walking softly, picking mushrooms gently, and placing them into baskets we had made from our untucked shirttails.

We return to that spot in the forest late each summer, always hopeful. Eighteen years have passed now. Although we have never again found chanterelles, we will always be hopeful and grateful that we once did.

WILD MUSHROOM TART

Eight first-course or six main-course servings

Ingredients:
Pastry dough
1 tablespoon unsalted butter
1 tablespoon vegetable oil
¾ pound mixed fresh wild mushrooms such as cremini, oyster, and chanterelle, quartered lengthwise
2 tablespoons finely chopped shallot
1 teaspoon chopped fresh thyme
¾ teaspoon salt
3/8 teaspoon black pepper
½ cup crème fraiche
½ cup heavy cream
1 whole large egg
1 large egg yolk

Special equipment: a 9- by 1-inch round fluted tart pan with a removable bottom; pie weights or raw rice.

Make shell: Roll out dough on a lightly floured surface with a lightly floured rolling pin into an 11-inch round and fit into tart pan, trimming excess dough. Chill until firm, about 30 minutes. Put oven rack in middle position and preheat oven to 375 degrees F. Lightly prick bottom of shell all over with a fork, then line with foil and fill with pie weights. Bake until side is set and edge is pale golden, 18 to 20 minutes. Carefully remove foil and weights and bake shell until bottom is golden, 10 to 15 minutes more. Cool completely in pan on a rack, about 15 minutes.

Make filling while shell bakes: Heat butter and oil in a 12-inch heavy skillet over moderately high heat until foam subsides, then sauté mushrooms, shallot, thyme, ½ teaspoon salt, and ¼ teaspoon pepper, stirring frequently, until mushrooms are tender and any liquid given off is evaporated, 8 to 10 minutes. Transfer to a bowl and cool to room temperature. Whisk together crème fraîche, heavy cream, egg, yolk, and remaining ¼ teaspoon salt and 1/8 teaspoon pepper in a medium bowl until combined.

Fill and bake tart: Reduce oven temperature to 325 degrees. Scatter mushrooms evenly in tart shell and pour custard over them. Bake tart in pan on a baking sheet until custard is just set and slightly puffed, 35 to 45 minutes. Cool tart in pan on rack at least 20 minutes, then remove side of pan. Serve tart warm or at room temperature.

RED FLANNEL HASH
AS MADE FOR THE HARVEST SUPPER AT THE
ADAMANT UNITED METHODIST CHURCH

We got this recipe from Kathi Doner and have modified it somewhat. It should feed at least 20 people--in any event it fills a large roasting pan.

You can either use ham or corned beef for this. We used ham for the harvest supper the last few years.

4 pounds corned beef or ham
6 quarts potatoes, peeled
and quartered

2 pounds onions, peeled and quartered
4 pounds carrots, cut into 3-inch pieces
1 - 2 heads of cabbage
2 turnips, peeled and quartered (optional)
beets

Bake or boil the beef or ham for about 30 minutes (until tender). Reserve the broth and cook potatoes, onions, carrots, cabbage, and turnips until tender. Reserve liquid. Boil beets separately.
Grind everything together. Add reserved liquid if too dry. No salt or pepper should be necessary.

If you make this dish one day ahead of serving it, the flavors will blend together nicely. Just remember that it will take about two hours to warm it properly. Warm it to 250 - 300 degrees F so the beets won't "bleed."

TARTIFLETTE

One of the joys of visiting or living in France is great food -- food that often demands lots of ingredients and lots of time. Tartiflette is a notable exception. It comes from the Haute Savoie region of France and is perfect for a cold winter's day. This means perfect on any given day for about six months out of an average year in Vermont. It is difficult to find true Reblochon cheese in the United States, but there are some worthy substitutes made right here in Vermont. Try, for example, Jasper Hill's washed-rind Willoughby or maybe even their Harbison or Winnimere. Also, be sure to use good local bacon.

Ingredients:
1 kilogram (about 2 ½ pounds) potatoes
1 wheel (1 pound) Reblochon cheese
6 slices (about ½ pound) bacon cut into small pieces
1 medium onion, finely chopped
170 milliliters (¾ cup) white wine
salt, pepper
1 knob (2 tablespoons) of butter or vegetable oil

Pre-heat the oven to 425 degrees F. (220 degrees C).

Boil potatoes, cool down, peel, and cut up into bite-sized pieces.

In a large frying pan, heat butter (or oil) and add onions. Saute slowly until golden brown. Add bacon and cook another 5 minutes. Now add the wine and prepared potatoes, season with salt and pepper, and cook over medium heat for about 10 minutes. Remove from the heat and put the potato mixture in an ovenproof dish.

Take the wheel of Reblochon, cut it in half across the wheel, and place both upper and lower halves on top of potato mixture.

Put in the oven and bake for about 20 - 25 minutes.

Enjoy with a glass of wine from the Savoie region of France.

TEMPLETON FARM BEEF & PARMESAN MEATBALLS

Templeton Farm is right up the road from the store, and Bruce and Janet Chapell are great neighbors who treat their bovine crew with kindness and respect. And their beef is great! These meatballs are easy to make. You can also use ground turkey, but then you'll need to bump up all of the flavoring, as turkey is really bland.

Yield: about 2 dozen medium meatballs.

Preheat the oven to 350 degrees F.

2 pounds grass-fed ground beef
3 large eggs
1 cup of grated parmigiano-reggiano (or more if you love parmesan as any reasonable person does)
½ cup bread crumbs (if you are eating gluten free you can do without them, but add more cheese then, to hold things together)
3 really large cloves pressed or finely chopped garlic (or more if you want)
2 tablespoons kosher salt
1 tablespoon ground black pepper
3 tablespoons dried basil. Or when it's in season, as much chopped fresh basil as you like!

Mix everything together in a big bowl. Use a fork so the mixture stays pretty loose. Line a large sheet pan with foil (or don't, if you like scrubbing pans or have dogs who can lick them clean).

Lightly form mixture into balls. Don't handle them more than necessary to hold together and get onto the pan. They are going to end up flat on the bottom anyway, so fussing over the shape will only make them tough. You can make them whatever size you want.
Place in rows on baking sheet. At five to a row I can fit all of them on one sheet (again, the not washing dishes theme).
Bake until done to your taste. I like them with some color on top. Somewhere around 20-25 minutes.
Eat plain or with any sauce you like.

BAKED SALMON STEAKS

According to Leighton Wass, who supplied this recipe, any type salmon can be used, including landlocked salmon from Lake Champlain or Lake Willoughby. He uses Atlantic salmon. He also is rather generous in sprinkling on the nutmeg.

2 salmon steaks about 1 inch thick
Juice of 1 lemon
Seasoned salt to taste
4 tablespoons of mayonnaise
Grated nutmeg
½ cup sliced fresh mushrooms
2 tablespoons grated parmesan cheese.

1. Grease a baking dish large enough that the steaks aren't touching.
2. Squeeze the lemon on each steak and sprinkle generously with seasoned salt.
3. Spread 2 tablespoons of mayonnaise over each steak and sprinkle lightly with nutmeg.
4. Top with mushrooms and parmesan cheese.

Bake uncovered at 400 degrees F for 15 minutes.
Serves 2.

BAKED WALLEYE FILLETS

Only a few places in Vermont have walleye (the Connecticut River, Lake Carmi, Lake Champlain). If you are lucky enough to catch some, here is a good recipe.

2 pounds walleye fillets
¼ cup butter
1 tablespoon Worcestershire Sauce
¼ cup chopped green onions
2 tablespoons lemon juice
1 clove minced garlic

Wash and dry fillets and place in a baking dish (glass).
Put ingredients in a sauce pan and bring to a boil.
Pour sauce over fillets. Bake for 35-40 minutes at 300 degrees F.

GRILLED FRESH VERMONT BROOK TROUT

There is some confusion about the name--it is Noyes Pond on some maps, but to locals such as Leighton Wass it is Seyon Pond, and we will not argue with him. He has registered to fly fish there over 200 times and has the certificate to prove it! According to Leighton, the brook trout for this recipe should be from Seyon Pond because they are native there and taste the best! If you can't get to Seyon Pond or have no luck there, use whatever brook trout you are lucky enough to catch. This recipe will feed two hungry fisherpersons.

3-4 freshly caught brook trout, cleaned, and 9-10 inches long
1 ¼ cups Panko bread crumbs (or white corn meal)
1 teaspoon crushed rosemary
1 teaspoon garlic pepper
2 tablespoons butter

1. Mix Panko, rosemary, and garlic pepper in plastic bag.
2. One at a time, place trout in bag and shake until well covered with the crumb mixture.
3. Place trout on aluminum foil with butter. Grill until they flake with a fork, about 8-10 minutes. (flip the fish over about half way through cooking)

Cooking sauce: 1 can coconut milk, 3 tablespoons soy sauce, 3 tablespoons rice wine vinegar 1 ½ tablespoons fish sauce (substitute soy sauce if desired). Crushed red chilies to taste. ¼ to 1 teaspoon.

I sometimes double the cooking sauce because any leftover is good by itself over rice.

In a wok (I use an iron skillet) heat oil and add onion, garlic, and ginger. Stir fry until soft. Remove. Briefly saute mushrooms. Remove and set aside with onion mixture. Stir fry chicken until slightly browned (only do enough at a time to have it cook quickly) Add oil as needed. Remove. Add cooking sauce and reduce down to about one third. Put everything back into skillet. Add basil and onions and heat through. Serve with rice.

THAI BASIL CHICKEN

2 pounds skinless boneless chicken breasts, cut into ¼ to ½ inch strips
6-7 mushrooms (crimini or shitake are nice) sliced
1 medium thinly sliced onion
3 cloves minced garlic
4 tablespoons minced fresh ginger
2-3 tablespoons peanut oil (or salad oil but peanut oil takes the heat best)
2 cups fresh basil, lightly chopped and packed
5 green onions cut into 1-inch pieces

JANET'S SPRING ROLLS

Sometimes called summer rolls, and if you want fresh herbs in Adamant, summer is better. Great to make when your garden herbs are flourishing. The vegetables used can be varied, but I always use carrots and lettuce. And mangos if they are available.

What to keep on hand: Rice paper, bean threads, rice wine vinegar, soy sauce. red chili pepper or hot chili oil
Fresh herbs: mint, basil, cilantro
Vegetables: carrots, lettuce, cucumber or zucchini, bean sprouts
Julienne carrots, cucumber or zucchini, mango

Cook bean threads in boiling water until just soft. They are thin and will cook very quickly so you need to watch over them. Drain and set aside.
Rice papers are prepared by dipping them in warm water and quickly removing. I place the rice paper on a wooden cutting board because the rice paper doesn't stick to it as it does to other surfaces. Do one at a time and then add the bean threads and veggies. Herbs can be chopped or laid in as whole leaves.
Lay filling materials on the bottom third of the rice paper. Pull edge up and roll tightly one roll, pull sides in over the roll like an envelope. Continue to roll until completely wrapped. Slice with vertical slice. Keep the rolls from touching each other or they will stick to themselves.
Dipping sauces: I make these up each time tasting and

varying ingredients until I like it. Here is one idea:
1 tablespoon tamari, 1 teaspoon dark sesame oil, 2 tablespoons rice vinegar, 1 tablespoon peanut oil, a dash or more of hot chili oil, 1/2 teaspoon minced garlic. Sprinkle with finely chopped peanuts. (You can also use lime juice instead of rice vinegar.
You can also make a peanut sauce: Mix together 1/2 cup peanut butter, 1/2 cup water, 2 tablespoons. soy sauce, 1 tablespoon brown sugar , 2 tablespoons peanut oil, 2 or 3 cloves minced garlic.

SPINACH DIP

1 package frozen, chopped spinach, thawed and squeezed dry
1 16-ounce container sour cream
1 cup mayonnaise
1 1.4-ounce package Knorr Vegetable recipe (soup) mix
1 8-ounce can water chestnuts, drained and chopped
3 green onions, chopped

Combine all ingredients and chill for at least 2 hours. Serve
with your favorite dippers.

KAY'S BLACKBERRY CORDIAL

1 quart (or more) ripe blackberries
1 cup sugar
1 liter vodka (100 proof is best for extracting flavor)

A large glass jar with a tight fitting lid (½-gallon mason jar works well)

Place blackberries in jar. Add sugar and pour vodka on top. Shake gently and leave in a place where you will remember to shake it (gently) each day for approximately 2 weeks. (You can let it sit longer if you wish, but usually the flavor is well extracted in two weeks).

Strain well (I use cheesecloth--doubled or tripled and rinsed in water, which keeps the cloth from absorbing the liquor.)

Put in Mason jars--or in decorative jars for gifts.

ALISON'S REFRESHING PUNCH

Mix together:
1 bottle pineapple juice
1 bottle peach, pomegranate, and/or raspberry juice
2-4 liters plain seltzer
Slice thinly a lemon and a lime
Add a few tops of mint
Let sit for at least an hour in fridge to absorb flavors and chill

STRAWBERRY LAVENDER JAM

1 pound of strawberries
1 pound sugar
2 dozen lavender stems with flowers
Juice of 2 lemons

Wash, dry and hull the berries. Layer them in a large bowl with the sugar and 1 dozen lavender stems and set in a cool place overnight. Discard the lavender and place the berry mixture in a large non-aluminum saucepan. Tie the remaining lavender stems together and add them to the berries. Add the lemon juice. Cook over medium heat until the mixture comes to a boil and then continue to cook for 20-25 minutes. Skim any foam from the top. Discard the lavender and pour the jam into sterilized jars.

Wonderful flavor with the lavender!!

MEXICAN DIP

1 cup sour cream
1 cup mayonnaise
1 envelope taco seasoning mix
1 avocado, peeled
¼ cup salsa
2 tablespoons lemon juice
¾ teaspoon hot sauce
1 can refried beans
6 ounces shredded cheddar cheese
2 chopped tomatoes
1 small can chopped olives

In a large, rectangular dish, mix can of refried beans and ½ tablespoon of hot sauce. Spread around.
In a bowl, mash avocado, stir in salsa, lemon juice, and ¼ teaspoon hot sauce. Spread on top of bean mixture.
In a bowl, mix sour cream, mayonnaise, and taco seasoning mix. Spread on top of avocado mix.
Sprinkle with cheese. Refrigerate overnight. Before serving top with tomatoes and olives.

COLESLAW

Ingredients:
1 cabbage, thinly sliced
4-5 carrots, grated
1 red onion, thinly sliced
1 bunch dill, chopped
1 cup mayonnaise
½ cup sour cream
¼ cup white wine vinegar
Salt to taste

Put vegetables in bowl.
Mix mayonnaise, sour cream, and vinegar together and pour over vegetables. Salt to taste. Leave in fridge for a couple of hours to let flavors mix together.

SAUERKRAUT

1 tablespoon bacon drippings
1 cup finely chopped onion
2 (16-ounce) packages sauerkraut, undrained
1 tablespoon packed brown sugar
1 teaspoon caraway seeds
½ cup chicken stock
½ cup cooking sherry

Directions
1. Heat bacon drippings in a large skillet over medium heat; Add onion and cook, stirring, until soft and translucent, about 5 minutes.
2. Place sauerkraut with juice into a large bowl and cover with water. Stir and use your hands to squeeze out as much of the water and juice as possible. Add squeezed sauerkraut to onion.
3. Stir brown sugar, caraway seeds, chicken stock, and cooking sherry into the sauerkraut mixture. Reduce heat to low and simmer until almost all the liquid has evaporated, 30 to 40 minutes, stirring occasionally.

APPLE BUTTER

Richard Czaplinski's apple butter recipe comes from the book "Putting Food By" by Ruth Hertzberg, Beatrice Vaughan and Janet Greene (page 340, called Old-style Apple Butter) but he modified it a bit. The secret is boiling the apples in apple cider and using apples that seem to capture that tangy apple flavor. Here's his modified recipe:

About 5 quarts of apples, unpeeled and quartered with stems and blossom ends (and cores if you like) taken out. Cook over low heat in several cups of apple cider. Process in food mill.

To the processed apple sauce, add spices (about a table-spoon of cinnamon, about a half teaspoon of ground cloves, about a half teaspoon of ground allspice). You'll need to experiment here to get the taste you like. Add some sugar to bring out flavor but not to make it too sweet (much less than recipes usually call for). You'll need to experiment here, too. Simmer over low heat for 2 hours or more. The butter will get thick and take on a darker color. It will splatter as bubbles pop out, so be careful. You'll need to stir the butter frequently so the bottom does not scorch.

Put the butter in jars (leave plenty of room as the butter will expand some in the bath) and process in a water bath. Be sure to leave the lids loose but closed. Bring bath to a boil and slow boil for about 10 minutes. Remove jars and tighten the lids, store and enjoy.

CHEESE CRACKERS

1 cup butter/margarine
1 pound sharp cheddar cheese, finely grated
2 ½ cups flour
1 teaspoon salt
1 teaspoon cayenne pepper
1 cup finely chopped pecans

Cream softened butter and finely grated cheese together
until smooth. Sift flour, measure, resift with salt and
pepper. Blend flour with cheese mixture. Add pecans.
Shape into 5 to 6 rolls (about 1-inch in diameter)
Wrap in wax paper. Chill. Slice thinly.
Bake at 375 degrees F for about 10 minutes.

FIDDLEHEADS

As was once the case with asparagus (which is now in
supermarkets almost year round), fiddleheads, the
still-curled fronds of the ostrich fern, are a sign of spring in
Vermont. And like asparagus, one of the best ways to
enjoy fiddleheads is to prepare them simply. Just be sure to
clean them well and cook them thoroughly.

Ingredients:
1 pound fresh fiddleheads (ends trimmed)
3 tablespoons olive oil
2 cloves of garlic (minced)
1 tablespoon lemon juice
salt, pepper

Bring a pot of salted water to a boil and blanch the fiddleheads (3 - 5 minutes). Drain.

Heat olive oil in a skillet or wok, add fiddleheads, garlic, salt
and pepper. Saute until the fiddleheads turn slightly brown
and are tender (around 5 minutes). Sprinkle with lemon
juice and serve.

CHICKEN, SPINACH, ETC., ON SPAGHETTI SQUASH

I modified this recipe from one I found on myrecipes.com
It has lots of ingredients but works with most things.
Modify as needed for what you have on hand.
Serves 4 as a one-dish meal.

Ingredients:
1 3-pound spaghetti squash
2 slices bacon
1 pound chicken breast
1/2 teaspoon salt, divided
1/2 teaspoon pepper, divided
1 1/2 cups onions
3 cloves garlic
1/2 red pepper (can use a spicier one if you want)
8 ounces mushrooms, white or baby bella
1/2 teaspoon oregano
1/2 teaspoon basil
1/2 cup white wine
1/4 cup spaghetti sauce
1/4 cup sun-dried tomatoes
1 cup chicken broth
6 ounces fresh baby spinach
1/2 cup cheddar cheese
1/4 cup parmesan cheese

1. Cut squash in half lengthwise and scoop out seeds. Place squash halves cut side down in a baking dish with 1/2-inch water. Bake at 400 degrees F for 1 hour, flipping the halves over with about 15 minutes to go. Scrape inside of squash with a fork to remove strands. Keep warm if done prior to the rest of it.
2. While squash is cooking prepare all ingredients for cooking:
Cut up chicken into bite-sized pieces and sprinkle with 1/4 teaspoon salt and 1/4 teaspoon pepper
Chop onion, garlic, pepper, mushrooms, sun-dried tomatoes and grate the cheese
3. About 25-30 minutes before the squash is done, start cooking the remaining ingredients:
Cook bacon over medium heat until crisp, drain on paper towel, and crumble.
Turn heat up a little, add chicken to drippings in pan and cook, stirring frequently about 4 minutes.
Remove chicken from pan and add onion to pan. May add 1 1/2 teaspoon oil to pan if needed.
Cook onion until soft (about 3 minutes),
Add remaining salt and pepper, red pepper, garlic, bacon, oregano, and basil and cook 1 minute.
Add mushrooms and cook an additional 4 minutes.
Add wine and cook an additional 3 minutes.
Add tomato sauce, cooked chicken, chicken broth, tomatoes, and spinach. Cook until spinach wilts, stirring constantly. Stir in cheddar cheese.
4. Place 1/4 of squash on each of 4 plates top each with 1/4 of topping and sprinkle with parmesan.

Every summer I go to Vermont, running away from the dreaded south Georgia/north Florida August heat. I rent a little camp on Curtis Pond in Maple Corner, and several times during my stay I walk from Maple Corner to Adamant. I have walked in rain and shine. It is a beautiful walk. I always think I am there before I actually arrive in Adamant. I see a bend in the road that I think is the last bend. I see what I think is Sodom Pond shining through the trees. But there is always another bend, and that shine is just a metal roof of a sugar house off in the woods. But finally there it is, the welcome squeak of the screen door, the friendly faces, the smell of warm scones. I buy a ginger beer and sit on the stone ledge and soak my poor old feet in the mill pond. The air is so clear, the grass so soft, the phlox so pink, the water so icy. I feel that I am in heaven on earth in Adamant.

--June White
Adamant Co-op member and
regular summer visitor
from Thomasville, Georgia

Co-op Specials

As soon as breakfast is over, people around here immediately start to think about lunch. Luckily for us, we have a licensed kitchen upstairs. That was not always the case.

The Co-op was founded in 1935 in a building that had been here for quite some time before that. Times change, and things that were accepted norms back then do not necessarily pass muster in the twenty-first century. And so it was that when we decided to open a kitchen, we learned that a licensed kitchen requires running water. The water running from the millpond to Sodom Pond in the brook across the road didn't meet the state inspectors' definition of "running." Despite what seemed like an insurmountable pile of red tape, and thanks to the generosity of neighbors, who gave us space to drill a well, we finally installed the plumbing, the running water, and the kitchen. Several years later we were licensed by the state, and since that day, we haven't stopped making food.

Beth Ann, who was one of the first cooks to use the Co-op kitchen, was a master at preparing good, fresh food. At the same time, we wanted to have food to go, food people could use to stock their freezers, food to take home when no one felt like cooking. So we spent some time figuring out what freezes well and came up with dishes such as chicken pot pie, macaroni and cheese, shepherd's pie, and empanadas.

Several times a month, crews of volunteers, each crew specializing in one dish, take over the upstairs kitchen and crank out that dish in quantity. Those dishes are offered as the daily special on the day of creation, and more often than not, they are eaten immediately or exit the Co-op that day for our customers' homes. What doesn't is packaged and frozen for sale at a later time.

We are extremely grateful to our volunteers--we really could not do this without them.

EMPANADAS

Whether they're called empanadas, pasteles, dumplings, knishes, egg rolls, bourekas, pierogies, pasties, samosas, or momos, just about every culture has a version of the all-in-one meal--dough filled with some sort of savory concoction. They can be held in the hand, carried in a lunch pail, eaten for dinner with fresh salsa. It takes nine of us to make the empanadas for the store. Chopping, mixing, rolling, stuffing, baking, bagging. A few overstuffed empanadas always burst out of their shells during the baking process and need to be eaten on the spot, piping hot. Hard job, but someone needs to do it.

Empanada Dough

Makes 8 tortillas

1 ½ cups white flour
1 cup masa harina
1 stick melted butter
1 teaspoon baking powder
1 teaspoon salt
6 ounces water
1 egg, slightly beaten, for glazing

Combine dry ingredients in food processor and pulse to blend. Add melted butter and blend. Add most of the water in a stream while processor is on until it pulls away from side of processor. Dump out and knead for just a few seconds to bring it all together. Form into a log shape and wrap in plastic or wax paper and chill for an hour.

Cut log into eight equal pieces. Press each piece flat using tortilla press. Using a rolling pin, roll out further to a 7-inch diameter circle, sprinkling more masa on each side to aid in rolling.

Tortillas can be filled or frozen for future use at this point. If freezing, put piece of wax paper between each one and freeze in a zip lock bag.

When filling empanadas, use a pastry brush to put beaten egg along the bottom edge of the half-circle where it will turn over to close (helps it to stick together). After filling, prick top of empanada with a fork in two or three places, then glaze with egg wash. Bake on a cookie sheet covered with parchment paper for about 20 minutes at 375 degrees F.

CHICKEN CHILE CHEESE EMPANADA FILLING
24 SERVINGS

2 tablespoons olive oil
4 cups yellow onions, finely diced
3 small cans diced green chiles with juice
1 jalapeno, seeded and finely diced
6 cloves minced garlic
3 tablespoons ground cumin
3 1/4 pounds chopped chicken breast (about 7.5 cups)
Juice from 2 limes
1 bunch chopped cilantro
7 cups grated sharp cheddar cheese (about 1 3/4 pounds)
1 tablespoon salt / 1/2 tablepsoon pepper

Saute onions until transparent. Add garlic for a minute at the end. (Also saute the onions and garlic for the pesto chicken recipe to save time. See page 69. If you do this, be sure to remove one third of the mixture and put it aside for the pesto chicken filling)
Add chiles to the sautéed onions and mix, then add other ingredients. Mix well. Add cilantro last.
Place in large zip lock bags and refrigerate (label bag) until you are ready to fill empanadas.

SWEET POTATO EMPANADA FILLING

4 cups frozen peas
4 tablepoons olive oil
4 cups diced sweet potato (about 1 1/2 to 2 large)
4 cups yellow onions, finely diced
8 ounces goat cheese
2 cups chopped cilantro
4 tablespoons Yemeni spice mix (see below)

Saute onions and sweet potato in oil, covered (adding small amount of water…1/2 cup approximately) until the potatoes are soft. Then uncover so water will evaporate. Use simmer burner. Roughly mash. Place in large pan. Add frozen peas and goat cheese. Mix, being careful to not mash the peas.
Add salt and spice mix. Mix gently and thoroughly.
Place in large bowl and cover with foil and refrigerate until you are ready to fill empanadas.

(YEMINI SPICE MIX: Equal amounts of cumin, black pepper, turmeric, and cardamom)

1 large sweet potato = approximately 2 1/2 cups; 1 large onion = approximately 2 cups.

PESTO CHICKEN EMPANADA FILLING

2-3 cups yellow onions, finely diced
3 cloves minced garlic
8 ounces grated mozzarella
8 cups chopped chicken breast
1 large bag (16 ounces total) frozen chopped spinach (defrost and squeeze out moisture)
1-2 16-ounce cans diced tomatoes (drained)
1 pound whole milk ricotta
3/4 cup (or to taste) Parmesan
4 heaping tablespoons basil pesto
1/2 tablespoon salt / 1/4 tablespoon pepper (or to taste)

Saute onions and garlic in a large pan (or use the onions and garlic that have been sautéed and set aside while making the chicken chile cheese filling. See recipe on page 68). Add all other ingredients (pesto, parmesan and salt and pepper last).
Place in large bowl and cover with foil unjtil ready to fill empanadas.

MACARONI AND CHEESE

1 ½ pounds pasta
½ pound of bacon
1 ½ sticks of butter
½ cup plus 1 tablespoon flour
8 ½ cups of milk
½ teaspoon nutmeg
½ teaspoon black pepper
½ teaspoon cayenne
½ tablespoon granulated garlic
10 cups grated extra sharp cheddar
½ bag of spinach
Topping:
½ stick butter
½ cup grated parmesan
½ cup panko crumbs

Melt butter, add panko and parmesan. Set aside.
Line sheet pan with tin foil. Put bacon on pan, put in cold
oven then turn up to 400 degrees F. Cook until crisp. Blot
and set aside. While the bacon is cooking, cook pasta
until al dente. Drain, pour cold water over it to
stop the cooking, then add a tad of olive oil
to prevent sticking. Put milk in large pot and
heat on low until warm. Melt butter in large pan.
Add flour and cook, stirring to remove
rawness from flour. While whisking butter
and flour, add warm milk slowly to
keep smooth.

Cook over medium heat whisking constantly until the
mixture bubbles and becomes thick, 20-30 minutes. It
needs to boil and thicken. Remove pot from heat, stir in
salt, nutmeg, pepper, cayenne, and all of the cheese and stir
until smooth.
Crumble bacon and add with chopped spinach. Stir. Add
pasta. Stir. Put mixture in pan and top with panko topping.
Broil just until nicely browned.

CHICKEN POT PIES
Yield: 32 pies

FOR THE FILLING
10 pounds diced chicken breast baked in 6 cups heavy cream
8 cups heavy cream (6 cups for baking the chicken and 2 cups for adding to the filling)
4 ½ pounds large carrots (14 cups), cut into small rounds or half rounds (they don't have to be peeled, just washed well)
2-pound bag frozen peas
4 ½ pounds yellow onions (14 cups), diced
1 ½ pounds butter
3 cups flour
9 cups chicken stock
5 tablespoons dried tarragon
2 tablespoons granulated garlic
6 teaspoons salt
1 tablespoons black pepper
5 tablespoons sherry

1. Get pot of water boiling.
2 Preheat the oven to 450 degrees F.
3. When water boils, dump in carrots and cook for 4 minutes. Drain and rinse in colander under cold water to stop cooking.
4. In large frying pan, melt butter over medium heat. Add onions and saute until translucent, about 10 minutes. Add flour and cook, stirring, for about 5 minutes. Make sure it doesn't stick to the bottom and does NOT brown.

5. Transfer onion-flour mixture to large pot and slowly add broth, stirring or whisking constantly to keep it from clumping. Then stir in reserved cooking juices, 2 cups cream, and the sherry. Keep stirring until thickened again and it begins to bubble.

6. Stir in tarragon, salt, pepper, and garlic and simmer 1 minute.

7. Add carrots, peas, and chicken and stir to incorporate everything.

8. Taste and adjust amounts of tarragon, salt, pepper, garlic, and sherry.

9. Spoon filling into tins, brush rim of tin with egg wash, put crust on tin, and crimp with a fork. Cut cross vents in top and brush with egg wash.

10. Put on foil-lined baking sheet and, when ready, put in oven and bake until brown.

FOR THE DOUGH (PATE BRISEE)

1 ½ cups flour
½ teaspoon salt
½ cup (1 stick) butter
¼ cup iced water

1. Put flour and salt in food processor and pulse to mix.

2. Cut cold butter into about 16 pieces and dump into processor. Pulse for about 1 minutes until it looks like coarse cornmeal.

3. While processor is running, stream in ice water slowly until dough begins to clump. It won't come together totally. It will look dry and weird. That's okay.
4. Dump mixture onto lightly floured board.
5. With the palm of your hand smooth dough bits firmly, pushing away from you. It will come together as the butter gets smooshed in. Then gather it together, push it into a ball, put it in a plastic bag, seal and put it in the fridge.
6. Depending on temperature in the room, take out ½ hour to 1 hour before using.
7. Roll out and cut using pie pan as template-make it about 1/8 inch larger all around.

CHICKEN PREPARATION

Preheat oven to 350 degrees F. If the chicken breasts are thick, slice in half flatwise. Place breasts on baking sheets with rims. Salt and pepper the chicken. Pour the 6 cups of cream over the chicken. Bake until juices run clear or the internal temperature reaches 170 degrees and there are no traces of pink. Remove chicken and reserve all liquid in a container. Dice chicken and remove all gristly and fatty bits.

SHEPHERD'S PIE with TWO TOPPING VARIATIONS

Okay, so here's the thing. According to the purists in the British Isles, what we call Shepherd's Pie is really Cottage Pie because REAL Shepherd's Pie is made with ground lamb, not beef. But the dish we all grew up with, often in school cafeterias, is made with beef and was called Shepherd's Pie, so that's our story and we're sticking with it. People have very strong feelings about what vegetables should be included: carrots, peas, corn. We've gone with the carrots and peas, but you can use anything you like. The key with Shepherd's Pie is to develop a deep, meaty, umami flavor. This takes experimentation. The flavoring here is different every time I make it. Add and taste, add and taste. Yield: 8 servings.

For the Filling:
2 pounds grass-fed ground beef (Templeton Farm)
2 large carrots, sliced medium thin
1 box frozen peas
1 large onion, diced
2 stalks celery, diced
3 large cloves garlic, pressed or finely chopped
2 tablespoons olive oil
1-2 tablespoons kosher salt
1-2 tablespoons ground black pepper
3-5 tablespoons tomato paste
2-4 tablespoons Worcestershire sauce
2-3 tablespoons dark soy sauce or mushroom soy sauce
About 2 cups chicken or beef stock (you want a good amount of gravy in the pie, so keep adding until the mixture is still thick, but juicy).

Saute onion, carrots, and celery with oil in a large covered pan over medium-low until the carrots are just tender. Add garlic and cook another minute or so. Don't burn the garlic. Remove veggies to a plate. Cook ground beef until all pink is gone. Pour off any fat. Put beef and veggies back in pot or pan. Add the rest of the ingredients in order, stirring and tasting after each addition. After you add the stock you'll need to add more flavor. Keep going until it has a really deep, beefy, flavor. Remember, it's going to need to hold up under a blanket of mashed potatoes, so make the flavors bold!

For the Topping:
about 5 pounds of either red potatoes or Yukon gold
OR
1 large butternut squash peeled and diced
About 1 cup heavy cream
1/2 cup butter
salt, pepper

Simmer potatoes or squash until tender. Drain and put in bowl. Mash or mix with heated cream and chopped butter. Salt and pepper to taste. This has to be spreadable on top of the meat, so it can't be too thick. Spoon the meat filling into a baking dish, or individual tins. Cover with as much potato or squash as you like. We pile it high. You'll need a spatula to spread it. Cover the meat entirely. With a fork, rough up the top. This will make nice browned bits. Bake in oven for about 20 minutes until hot. If the tops aren't browned, turn the broiler on high for just a few minutes.

EVA'S CURRIED CHICKEN SALAD

5 pounds boneless chicken breasts, baked, roasted, however you want to cook them. I usually cook mine in heavy cream (½ pint for the 5 pounds), a bit of granulated garlic, some salt, and some pepper. I cook it at 325 degrees F until done.

Then let the chicken cool. When cooled, trim off any fat and gristle and chop however fine you like.

DRESSING

3 ½ cups mayonnaise
2 tablespoons Muchi curry powder (or whatever curry powder you prefer)
2 teaspoons fresh lemon juice
2 teaspoons kosher salt
2 teaspoons granulated garlic (NEVER garlic powder or garlic salt!)
1-2 tablespoons apricot preserves
1 teaspoon maple syrup

Whisk all ingredients together really well

Add and stir well:

1 finely diced medium red onion
1 cup dried cranberries
1 cup lightly toasted pecans, chopped roughly

You can substitute chopped, dried apricots for the cranber-

ries, and slivered almonds for the pecans if you want. Adjust the heat or sweetness to your own preferences.

QUESADILLAS

Basically, what can go wrong with fried bread and cheese of any kind? These are a great way to dispose of leftovers. Use your imagination!

Ricardo and Maria's Tortillas--I use the large ones. These are particularly good tortillas but you can use any you like. Grated or sliced cheese--I like the combination of sharp cheddar and mozzarella, but you can use anything.
Thinly sliced onion
Diced red, yellow, or orange bell peppers
Fresh spinach
Your favorite salsa--either store bought or home made

Heat a large, dry frying pan. Have all of your ingredients ready to go. Place a tortilla in the pan for a minute and then flip it. Put on cheese (don't be stingy), then onion, pepper, spinach, and salsa. I used a slotted spoon for the salsa so it doesn't get too wet, on lower half of tortilla. Fold top half over it. Press down lightly with spatula.

Cook on one side until brown, then flip, using spatula and fingers (try not to burn yourself) so it doesn't spill its ingredients, and cook on other side until brown and cheese has melted.

BLACK FLY FESTIVAL, COOKOUT, AND OTHER SPECIAL EVENTS FAVORITES

The winter months are long and often lean at the Co-op. It is special fund raisers at other times of the year that allow us to survive. Some of these events have become seasonal institutions.

Take the Black Fly Festival, for example. It all started at a Co-op board meeting when, during a discussion of how to breathe new life into the summer fair, Cindy Cook launched into an ear-blistering rant about the black flies of springtime. "What a great idea," someone said--and the first Black Fly Festival was born. That was 2003. It naturally had to take place in May, so that the black flies would be in a feeding frenzy. It had to have food, music, and a parade. The most recent "BFF" kicked off with a nature walk through prime blackfly habitat around Sodom Pond and continued with lots of music; food, food, and more food; a Black Fly Festival pie contest; a fashion show the likes of which New York and Milan shall never see; a poetry slam; and a silent auction -- you know, the usual.

On another occasion, board members were again casting about for a possible fundraiser. The board asked itself what the community would like, and Rick Barstow came up with Friday night grilling. The Friday night cookouts started out under tarps stretched tight overhead with just hot dogs and hamburgers and approximately 25 people huddled beneath. They have since evolved into a somewhat more civilized dining experience under a proper canopy. There are still the obligatory jumbo hot dogs and hamburgers, but also .

salmon burgers, assorted salads, desserts, and specials such as pulled pork, wings, or pizza. On a typical Friday now about 75 people show up, very nearly equal to the entire population of Adamant.

In early October, at peak foliage time, we serve a traditional English Cream Tea in Janet's studio above the Co-op store. There one may sit drinking tea (or coffee, if you prefer) eating fresh scones with a dollop of Adamant-made clotted cream and strawberry jam, and, of course, cucumber sandwiches, surrounded by Janet's paintings and a panoramic view of Sodom Pond. We challenge you to find a better cream tea outside of Devon or Cornwall!

A few years ago, an astonished Co-op clerk beheld Seth and Erika walking into the Co-op dressed in black tie and evening gown and looking for whipped cream. It was their anniversary and they said they were going to celebrate it canoeing the pond and eating strawberries and cream. The next year the couple was joined by Eva and Janet, and the Adamant Dinner Cruise was born. Each year since, more people have flocked to the water--dressed up, dressed down, in canoes, kayaks, in homemade contraptions barely able to stay afloat, each with a buoyant pot luck dinner to share. Only in Adamant... (to our knowledge, at least).

We also love desserts in Adamant, so much so that we devote one evening a year to them and have given them a special place in this book.

EVA'S DEVILED EGGS

Eggs
Hellman's mayonnaise
Grey Poupon (Dijon style) mustard
Salt
Pepper
Paprika

1. Peeling the eggs is the hard part. They don't have to be perfect, but sometimes they are really stubborn. The fresher the eggs are, the harder they will be to peel.
2. Boil eggs. You want, as much as possible, to preserve the beautiful orange color of the yolk, so it's important not to overcook. I put the eggs in warm water. Bring them to a boil and turn the fire off as soon as they boil. Then let them sit for 7-8 minutes.
3. Plunge them into a bowl filled with really cold water and keep the water running for a few minutes so it stays cold. Then peel as soon as possible.
4. Cut eggs in half, dumping yolks in a small bowl. Add Hellman's mayonnaise (the healthy alternatives just don't hack it for deviled eggs!) Grey Poupon mustard, salt, and pepper

The amounts are totally up to you. The filling should end up creamy, and there should be a real kick from the mustard. Start off slow with the mustard (maybe a teaspoon for 6 eggs, and then add to taste)

Fill whites with mixture and sprinkle with paprika.

KATHI'S DEVILED EGGS

1 dozen eggs
Mayonnaise
Dill
Salt

If you are using local, farm fresh eggs -- put them in the fridge for about one week. This will make peeling the eggs sooooo much easier!

Hard boil the eggs, peel, and cut in half. Take out the yolk and mash. Add mayonnaise to get the taste and texture you like. Season with dill and salt. Pipe mixture into egg halves.

Serving
by Janet Pocorobba

I help out at the suppers,
serve Helen's Mississippi Mud brownies
and Donna's carrot cake.
I stand to serve,
Janet, cool and unbound, shows
her sketches of Scotland.
I dip into trays:
Are my slices too big, too crumbly? Shall
I offer or hawk? Be myself or a waitress,
polite or saucy? Gary Anne is taking
photos at the pond.
Looking, capturing, preserving.
Art as a way of interacting with the
world. Step aside,
adopt a medium,
something between you and
the environment.
Engage.
Piano like rain in the trees.
She's deep in with her zoom lens.
Matt, from the music school, I'd seen
him looking at turtles before
in cap and green tee, comes out to talk.
Even he takes her camera,
points, shoots.
At the cookout, flies around my head
won't leave me alone.
Oh, take heart and serve.
It's just a piece of pie.

PULLED PORK

This is easily the best pulled pork recipe I have ever had. I found it in the Times Argus (June 9, 2009). It is from Jimmy Kennedy , who owned the River Run cafe in Plain-field, Vermont.

For the rub:

3 tablespoons sugar
1 tablespoons brown sugar
2 tablespoons salt
2 tablespoons ground cumin
2 tablespoons ground black pepper
2 tablespoons chili powder
4 tablespoons paprika
½ teaspoon cayenne pepper

5 pounds pork shoulder (Boston butt)
3 cups of your favorite BBQ sauce

Make the rub (put all ingredients in a jar and mix togeth-er).
Preheat the oven to 250 degrees F (121 degrees C).
Trim pork of fat.
Line a baking pan large enough to hold the pork with heavy-duty aluminum foil.
Put the meat in the pan and sprinkle evenly with about ½ cup of the rub.

Cover the pan with a tent of heavy-duty aluminum foil, folded over the edges to seal it.
Roast 8 - 9 hours. You know it's done when you poke the meat with a fork and it falls off the bone. Shred the meat.
Heat BBQ sauce and mix with the meat.
Enjoy!

Pizza!

The allure of singed dough, bubbling cheese, tomato, and basil trumps all. We've made pizza in January, tripping over three-foot snow drifts. We've made pizza in July, when no sane person would stand at the mouth of an inferno. The first time we fired up the clay oven, a couple of us lost our eyelashes, and the oven door burst into flames, necessitating a fiery dash to the brook across the road. It's all worth it! And there's no need to worry about calculating pizza amounts: it doesn't matter whether you are serving 25, 50, or 100. They will eat as much pizza as there is.

"COOKOUT" PIZZA

FOR THE DOUGH:

1 package active dry yeast
1 teaspoon sugar
1 cup warm water
2 tablespoon kosher salt
2 tablespoons extra-virgin olive oil
3 cups 00 (double zero) flour, plus more for dusting
(I use Caputto flour or King Arthur "Italian" flour)

The directions here are for using a mixer with a dough hook but, of course, you can do this by hand, too.

Mix warm water and sugar in bowl of mixer. Add yeast and let stand for 10 minutes to proof. Add salt and oil.
Add 2 cups of the flour to begin with and start the mixer on low with dough hook (otherwise you'll get flour all over the kitchen). Gradually add the rest of the flour. Turn out onto floured board and knead until it all comes together and as smooth as a baby's bottom. If it sticks to the board add a bit more flour, but this should be a fairly wet dough.

Cover with a dry towel and allow to rise for about 1 ½ hours until doubled. Punch down and shape into as many balls as you want, depending on the desired size of pies. Put balls on tray, cover with towel and allow to rest for about half an hour before rolling out.

SAUCE:

Simply take a large can of good Italian tomatoes and dice and add a bit of salt.

The pizzas at the cookout are made with tomatoes, pesto, mozzarella, chopped garlic, and parmigiano-reggiano cheese.

If you don't have a pizza oven, then get the oven as hot as possible, and use a pizza stone if you have one.

Community Oven

It began with a foundation of the same stones that support Vermont's fields. Then came sand and saplings, bales of straw, and river clay. At the end of the day it was a wood-fired oven, but that didn't make it a community oven. It wasn't until Gail England, who organized and oversaw the construction as part of Transition Town Montpelier's "Villagebuilding Convergence" started a clay tendril winding up one side of the oven. Over the next few days more clay tendrils appeared, along with clay frogs and clay sunflowers, put there by people who came by to see the oven and were inspired to add their own touch. That's when it became a community oven.

SUMMER BERRY SALAD WITH CREAMY RASPBERRY DRESSING

2 cups mayonnaise
2/3 cup granulated sugar (can use less if desired)
1/3 cup half & half
1/3 cup raspberry vinegar
2-3 tablespoons seedless raspberry jam
2 tablespoons poppy seeds
2-3 hearts of romaine lettuce leaves (or mixed greens, if preferred), torn into pieces, washed in cold water, drained well
1 pint fresh firm strawberries, hulled and sliced lengthwise
1 small red onion, halved and thinly sliced
1 cup fresh blueberries
¼ cup slivered almonds, toasted (optional)
Feta cheese, crumbled

Directions: (Note – this makes a large amount of dressing and leftover can be refrigerated for up to week.)

Prepare the dressing first so you can chill it before serving. In medium size mixing bowl, combine the first six ingredients and mix well (or use a food processor). Cover and chill well.

A couple of hours before serving, prepare the lettuce as directed. Layer lettuce on very large serving plate (or use a large bowl). Add amount of desired dressing and toss well. Layer berries, almonds, onions, and feta on top.

GRILLED PORTABELLA MUSHROOMS

Incredibly simple. Great on the grill in the summer, but also fine under the broiler.

Portabella mushrooms (one medium or large per person)
Balsamic vinegar
Olive oil
Granulated garlic
Kosher salt
Black pepper

Wipe mushrooms off with a paper towel.
Remove stems.
Pre-heat grill or broiler to medium.
Place mushrooms, gill side up, on baking sheet lined with foil. Sprinkle each mushroom liberally with olive oil--they will absorb quite a bit (maybe 2 tablespoons or so).
Sprinkle each mushroom with balsamic vinegar--about half as much as the oil. Sprinkle with a lot of granulated garlic. Mushrooms can take quite a bit--maybe 1 tablespoon per mushroom. Salt and pepper to taste.

Place under broiler or on grill, until top side softens. Then flip over and cook until tender but not mushy.

Options: When they are done you can add some roasted red pepper and goat cheese and place back on the grill or under the broiler for a couple of minutes.

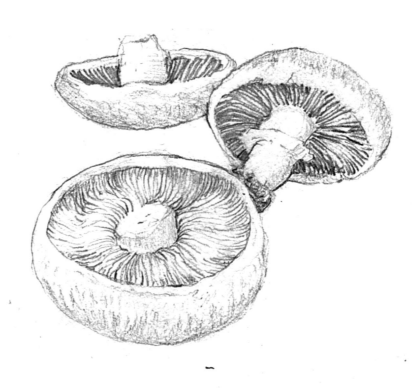

Adamant Tonight
By Ron Padgett

Every Friday in summertime, in mid-afternoon, a particular aroma comes to my mind and then vanishes. It is a brief memory, but it is enough to evoke the image of a foot-long wiener, glistening and slightly charred, held aloft for a moment in a pair of silver tongs before it comes to rest in a bun. I turn to my wife and say, "Adamant tonight," to which she replies, "You don't have to remind me." And so we fritter away the next few hours, glancing at our watches from time to time, until the moment of departure arrives. We time our leaving so we will arrive early enough that the supply of our beloved hot dogs will not have been exhausted by—horrors—a sudden influx of surprise visitors with a culinary desire equal to ours. With our hot dogs loaded with mustard and relish and accompanied by two lovingly homemade side dishes and a bottle of cream soda or sarsaparilla, we find an empty table and fall to eating, to be joined by whatever friends happen to arrive. As part-time residents, we don't know everyone in the community, but the atmosphere at the cookout is so familial and civilized and downright pleasant that we--grim Manhattanites for seven months of the year--relax into it with a special pleasure. When the dining and the leisurely talk are finally done I walk to our car with the comforting premonition that next Friday, in mid-afternoon, a certain aroma will again come to my mind and I will begin to salivate.

CHEESE-STUFFED BAKED POTATOES

This is not health food. What makes the potatoes great is adding ridiculous amounts of cheese, butter and sour cream.

8 large russet or Idaho potatoes
Seriously sharp cheddar cheese, grated--about 8 ounces
Sour cream--about a cup
Butter--about one stick, cut into small pieces
Granulated garlic-about 1 teaspoon
Fresh or dried chives--however much you like
Salt to taste
Pepper to taste

1. Bake potatoes at 400 degrees F until done.
2. Put the grated cheese, sour cream, and butter in the bottom of a bowl.
Scoop the hot potato insides into the bowl so the heat melts everything. Be careful not to tear the potato skins. Stir with a fork, leaving some texture, but no huge potato chunks.
3. Add seasonings to taste.
4. Refill potato skins and place on baking sheet.
5. Put under broiler on high for just long enough for tops to begin to brown.

ERIN'S POTATO SALAD

10 pounds red-skinned potatoes cut into roughly equal
size pieces, covered with boiling water, and cooked until
just tender, not mushy
4-5 ribs of celery, diced small
5-6 green onions, diced small
½ cup plus finely chopped parsley
¼ cup finely chopped thyme
1 cup mayonnaise
1 cup plain yogurt
6 tablespoons cider vinegar (or to taste)
1 tablespoon Dijon-style mustard (or to taste)
Salt and pepper
1 cup fresh English peas or roughly chopped
sugar snap peas or thawed peas
(previously frozen)

Dressing:
Combine mayonnaise, yogurt, herbs, vinegar, mustard,
onions, and pepper. Whisk together. Cool the cooked
potatoes. Dice cooled potatoes to bite sized, removing
some of the skins (many fall off by themselves). For such a
large recipe, salt and pepper the potatoes in layers in a large
bowl and incorporate dressing, celery, and peas gently so
not to mash potatoes.

PAT'S CURRIED BROCCOLI SALAD WITH RED GRAPES AND CHUTNEY DRESSING
Makes 15 servings

2 heads broccoli (or use 1 head broccoli and 1 head cauliflower)
5 cups seedless red grapes
½ cup chopped red onion
Dressing:
½ cup light mayonnaise
½ cup light sour cream
1 cup light or fat free plain yogurt
2 tablespoons curry powder
3 tablespoons chutney

Chop broccoli finely. Halve grapes. Put broccoli, grapes, and onion in a bowl. Mix together dressing ingredients and stir into broccoli mixture.

CORN SALAD

Adapted from "Edible Green Mountains" publication by Lucy Wollaeger.

4 or 5 ears of corn (or frozen equivalent)
1 red onion, chopped
1 sweet red pepper, chopped
Several stalks of celery, chopped
Fresh basil or cilantro
3 tablespoons olive oil
2 tablespoons apple cider vinegar
1 tablespoon lemon juice (optional)
Salt and pepper
Black beans and Greek olives (optional)

Cook corn in boiling water for 3 minutes, (or prepare frozen corn as instructed on package). When cool, cut kernels off cobs. Combine with other ingredients. Chill. Serves 4.

ANTIPASTO KABOBS

Bamboo skewers (10-inch skewers will hold approximately 10-12 ingredients)

Customize the skewer to your liking with the ingredients listed below, using all or just a few. Start and end with something that won't be likely to 'slip' off the ends (tomatoes are good starters/enders) (I alternate as follows: tomato, mozzarella ball, black olive, meat, tortellini, and then repeat times two) for each skewer.

Suggested foods for layers:
Mozzarella balls
Grape or cherry tomatoes
Black pitted olives
Green olives
Cheese tortellini (pre cook per package directions...do not overcook!)
Italian meats cut into bite sized chunks (genoa salami, soppressata, prosciutto)
Artichoke hearts

Drizzle with Pesto Dressing (see below) a couple of hours before serving or use a vinaigrette of your choice.

Pesto Dressing:
Mix well
3/4 cup olive oil
1 packed cup of chopped basil
2 minced garlic cloves
1/2 - 1 cup parmesan cheese

You may also combine the tortellini, cheese, and tomatoes in a bowl and drizzle the dressing on them first for an hour or more before skewering them.

ORZO VEGGIES

I adapted this recipe to a salad by just boiling the orzo and chilling it with the roasted veggies. Roast the vegetables on a cookie sheet, then chill. Boil orzo, then chill. Mix together.

1 pound asparagus, trimmed
3 bell peppers (red, green, and yellow)
4 green onions, chopped
1 cup grape tomatoes, halved
1 medium zucchini
4 tablespoons olive oil, divided
1 garlic clove, crushed
1 tablespoon Italian seasoning
3/4 teaspoon salt
1/8 teaspoon coarsely ground pepper
1 cup orzo

Preheat oven to 350 degrees F.
Cut vegetables into bite-sized pieces.
Place first five ingredients in a 13 x 9-inch baking dish. Add 2 tablespoons olive oil, garlic, seasonings, salt, and pepper. Toss well. Roast 30 minutes or until veggies are tender. Add remaining 2 tablespoons olive oil to large saucepan. Add orzo and saute until brown. Add broth, bring to boil, reduce heat to low, and cook, covered, until liquid is absorbed. Add orzo to roasted veggies and mix. Sprinkle with pine nuts and cheese on top. Cover with foil and bake 30 minutes. Serves 8

KAREN'S WHEAT BERRY SALAD WITH PEACHES

(from Clean Food)

1 ½ cups wheat berries
Sea salt
4-5 scallions, chopped
1 cup chopped peaches (apples are a nice substitute in fall)
½ cup currants
¼ cup toasted sunflower seeds
juice of 1 lime
3 tablespoons toasted sesame oil

Rinse wheat berries, soak in bowl with enough water to cover for 2 hours, then drain. In large pot, bring 3 ¼ cups water to boil. Add wheat berries and a pinch of salt, reduce heat, cover, and simmer until all water is absorbed (35-45 minutes). Set aside to cool, then fluff with fork.

In large bowl, combine cooked wheat berries with scallions, peaches, currants, and toasted sunflower seeds. Toss with lime juice, toasted sesame oil, and pinch of salt. Serve at room temperature or chilled.

For a change, substitute your favorite vinaigrette for the sesame oil and lime juice. To make this salad gluten free, use wild rice instead of wheat berries.

Serves 8

ALMA'S POTATO SALAD VERDE

6 medium yellow potatoes
6 medium scallions, finely sliced
2 stalks celery, finely sliced
1 small yellow onion, finely sliced
2 jalapeno peppers, chopped
1 tablespoon fresh dill, chopped
1 tablespoon fresh lemon balm
4 hard-boiled eggs
3 medium sour pickles, chopped
8 pimento-stuffed green olives, thinly sliced
1 tablespoon fresh marjoram, minced
mayonnaise
1 teaspoon salt
1 teaspoon sugar
freshly ground pepper to taste

Boil potatoes until tender (about 25 minutes). Let cool.
Peel. Cut into cubes.
Place all ingredients, except mayonnaise, in a bowl and
gently mix.
Add mayonnaise to taste. Mix until all ingredients are
coated.
Chill salad for two hours before serving.

AMY'S CLASSIC POTATO SALAD

2 pounds potatoes
1 cup mayonnaise
1 tablespoon Dijon mustard
2 tablespoons vinegar
1 1/2 teaspoons salt
1/4 teaspoon ground black pepper
Chopped fresh parsley (to taste)
1 cup diced celery

Cover potatoes with water and bring to a boil. Reduce heat
to low and simmer until potatoes are tender. Drain and
cool slightly. Peel if desired. Cut into cubes as desired.
Combine mayonnaise, mustard, vinegar, parsley, salt, and
pepper in large bowl. Add potatoes, celery, and toss gently.
Serve chilled or at room temperature.

ALISON'S TABBOULEH

1 cup medium bulgur
1 cup mint, diced fine (I particularly like apple mint, the tall, slightly fuzzy kind, that is quite minty without the sharp taste and feel of the smaller spearmint, although this can be used also)
3 cups parsley, diced fine
3 cups chopped tomatoes, drained
1 large clove garlic, chopped fine
1 large onion, chopped
½ cup scallions, chopped
¼ cup lemon juice
½ cup low salt V-8 or other vegetable juice
¼ cup water
Pinch of pepper
4–6 tablespoons good olive oil

Heat the lemon juice, vegetable juice, and water to almost boiling. Pour over bowl of bulgur (should be approx. ¼ inch above the grains), stir, cover, and let stand for approximately 30 minutes. While the bulgur is absorbing the liquids, chop your vegetables and herbs and toss together. Bulgur should absorb all the liquid and be light and fluffy when forked. If there is still too much liquid, drain. Add chopped vegetables and herbs. Add pepper and some olive oil. Spoon onto some fresh lettuce and serve.
For a special treat that will wow your friends, stuff some tabbouleh into some fresh day lilies.

Day lilies are edible and look lovely on your dinner platter.

Options: Add chopped green pepper, cucumber, zucchini. If you are a salt lover either use salted vegetable juice or add coarse salt to taste. Use cous cous instead of bulgur.

WILD RICE ARABIAN NIGHTS SALAD

2/3 cup uncooked wild rice
½ cup brown rice
3 cups water
1 teaspoon salt
2 whole chicken breasts
½ cup olive oil
¼ cup lemon juice
1 cup chopped parsley
½ cup green onions
1 tablespoon dried mint leaves
½ pint cherry tomatoes, quartered

In medium saucepan, wash rice with warm tap water, drain in strainer (I've never done that).
Return rice to pan, add water and salt. Bring to a boil, cover, and cook over low heat 75-90 minutes until water is absorbed. Meanwhile, broil chicken or boil chicken in water until tender, cool slightly. Cut chicken in julienne strips or cubes. In large bowl, combine wild rice, chicken, oil, lemon juice, parsley, onions, and mint. Cover and refrigerate until cold. Just before serving, add tomatoes and toss gently. Garnish with lemon wedges if you wish. Serves 4-6 (as a main course).

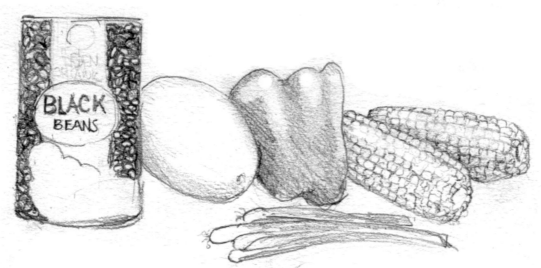

AMY'S BLACK BEAN MANGO QUINOA SALAD WITH CILANTRO LIME VINAIGRETTE

4-6 servings

1 ½ cups dry quinoa
1 can black beans, drained and rinsed (or 2 cups cooked)
1 mango, diced
1 red pepper, diced
1 ½ cups corn (fresh or frozen)
1 cup scallions, diced
Salt and pepper to taste

(Note: you can mix and match different vegetables here - cucumbers, tomatoes, carrots, zucchini, asparagus, peas, different colored peppers, etc.)

For the dressing:
1/3 cup lime juice
2 tablespoons extra virgin olive oil
1 cup fresh cilantro
1 garlic clove
½ teaspoon salt
Pepper to taste
Cumin to taste if you wish

In a sauce pan, combine quinoa with 3 cups of water, bring to a boil, then reduce the heat to medium and let quinoa cook for about 15 minutes or until all the water is absorbed. Let quinoa cool to room temperature. Add the beans, mango, and vegetables to the cooled quinoa. Salt and pepper to taste. Make dressing by putting all ingredients into a food processor, blender, or with a hand blender until thoroughly blended. Pour dressing over salad and serve.

SPINACH AND KALE GRATIN

Serves 8

2 pounds Lacinato kale (remove stems and chop leaves)
1 pound young spinach leaves
2 tablespoons unsalted butter
4–6 slices of good bread (enough to make 1 ½ cups of
bread crumbs (Red Hen Ciabatta or Cyrus Pringle is great)
½ cup grated Parmigiano-Reggiano cheese
Oil for sautéing
½ cup chopped onion
2 tablespoons flour
½ cup warmed heavy cream
1 ¼ cups warmed half and half
½ cup grated smoked Gouda cheese
Salt, pepper, nutmeg

1. Preheat oven to 400 degrees F and butter casserole
dish (I use a 2-inch deep round dish that is 10 inches
or so in diameter).
2. Toast bread slices and then put in food processor to
chop into coarse crumbs. Mix in small bowl with the
Parmigiano-Reggiano.
3. Sauté the chopped kale leaves in oil. Remove from pan
and put in large bowl and then sauté spinach leaves.
Remove spinach and squeeze out excess moisture by
pressing against side of a colander. Add to kale.
4. Sauté onion in butter until soft. Add flour and stir for
one minute. Whisk in cream and half and half slowly.
Continue to stir or whisk until moderately thickened
(about 2 or 3 minutes).

5. Add the cream mixture to the spinach and kale and then
add the Gouda cheese. Season with salt, pepper, and a pinch
or two of nutmeg. Mix all together gently with a spoon.
6. Pour into casserole dish. Top with bread crumb mixture.
7. Bake at 400 degrees F until bubbly and browned slightly
on top – about 30 minutes.

BEAN HOLE BAKED BEANS

This recipe came from Lois Toby (1926 – 2015), who grew up in Adamant and went to school at the one-room school house that is now the Adamant Community Club. The building is maintained by the Community Club, which held a Chicken Barbeque and Bean Hole Bean Dinner as the main fundraiser for years. Lois was also our beloved village matriarch, former postmistress, and the keeper of photos and the memorabilia that is our history. This recipe will easily feed the Grand Army of the Republic. You'll probably want to adjust the recipe amounts accordingly for a smaller group.

40 pounds of beans (yellow eyes or soldiers)
6 cups white sugar
6 cups dark brown sugar
12-ounce jar molasses
2 gallons dark maple syrup
13 1/2 tablespoons salt
6-2/3 tablespoons dry mustard
1-2/3 tablespoon pepper
20 onions (sliced or use a food processor)
10 pounds salt pork (cut in 1-inch pieces)

Soak beans overnight. In the morning, drain off water and add fresh. Boil until tender. Add a pinch of baking soda 5 minutes before the beans are done.

Mix sugar, molasses, maple syrup, salt, pepper, and dry mustard together. Set aside.

Mix beans, onions, salt pork, and the above mixture in a large stainless steel container with a tight lid, cover beans well with water, put on cover. Heat the bean mixture in the pot. It needs to go into the hole hot. Bake in ground at least 24 hours (see instructions for the bean hole that follow).

Hint: Cover the outside of the container with dish detergent, then with aluminum foil. Makes clean up easier.

Preparing the Bean Hole

The size of the bean hole depends on the size of your pot. The hole should be big enough around to have a 6-inch space between the pot and the edge of the hole on all sides. To help hold heat, put some softball-sized stones in the hole before starting the fire or add them to the fire while it is burning.

Start a fire in the hole using seasoned hardwood and keep it filled with good dry hardwood. Let it burn for about 3 hours. The hole should be at least 3/4 full of hot coals. Using a long-handled spade or shovel, shovel the coals out of the hole, leaving about 3 inches of live coals in the bottom of the hole. Set the bean pot in the hole on top of the 3-inch bed of coals. Shovel the rest of the coals around and on top of the pot. Cover with dirt and check for escaping steam, making sure none is leaking out. If steam is leaking out, cover area with more dirt. Leave the pot in the ground for 8 hours or overnight. Note: Make sure the beans are completely covered with hot water before putting them in the ground. The beans need to go into the ground hot.

Stirred
by Liz Benjamin

Kick the snow off your boots
Greet the papier-mache pigs and cats
Feel the hug of the glowing wood stove
Grab some bread, some wine, your mail
"What about that movie?"
"Your leg any better?"
"See those wild turkeys?"
"Great guitar work last night."
Potatoes, ideas,
onions, opinions,
spices, hopes,
worries, soup,
stirred together in the Co-op stew

CHOCOLATE AND OTHER DESSERTS

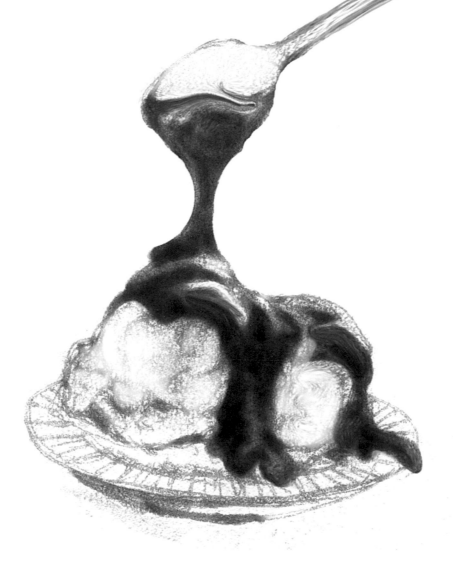

Desserts -- what is there to say? -- here in Adamant we love sugar -- and we love chocolate. The more desserts the better! We even devote one evening a year to desserts, the "Decadent Desserts and Wine Tasting" near Valentine's Day in February. The Co-op store is atmospherically transformed with lanterns and other lights, and the harsh fluorescents, subdued with yellow paper, cast a warm glow to match the cozy warmth of the wood stove. Hearts abound, even on the front steps, where Janet arranges Valentine hearts of ice. Stout cake, flourless chocolate cake, mascarpone cheese cake, profiteroles with raspberry sauce and chocolate, brownies, cookies, and more adorn the main counter, and a small variety of wines for sampling are arranged on the checkout counter by the register..It doesn't matter how cold it is outside (and it can be very, very cold in Vermont in the middle of February!)—inside the store it is toasty and hearts are warm.

Needless to say, after such an extravaganza in February, we also love walking, running, cycling, and aerobic black fly swatting during the warmer months.

On the following pages we share with you some of the wonder-fully magical and decadent desserts we love so much.

ANGEL MOCHA PIE

Our great grandmother, Winifred (Winnie) Wass, would make this pie for her Bridge Club. It was very popular then and it still is!
-Janet and Leighton Wass

Crust:
3 egg whites
¼ teaspoon cream of tartar
¾ cup sugar
Dash of salt

Beat whites until really stiff, but not dry, adding sugar and cream of tartar gradually. Beat until stiff and shiny. Spread on sides and bottom of well greased 8-inch pie plate. Bake at 275 degrees F for 1 hour.

Filling:
12-ounce package chocolate tidbits
¼ cup light Karo (corn) syrup
¼ cup water
1 tablespoon instant coffee granules (mash up fine)
3 egg yolks
1 cup heavy cream, whipped
1 teaspoon vanilla

Melt tidbits over hot (not boiling) water. Remove from heat. Combine Karo syrup and water and add to melted tidbits. Beat in coffee and egg yolks one at a time Fold in whipped cream and vanilla.

Pour into cooled meringue shell.
Chill in 'fridge
Lick all utensils clean!

Optional:
Whip more cream and mix with chocolate powder until a color suitable to your liking. Spread over the top of filling and add chocolate shavings to top.

FLOURLESS CHOCOLATE CAKE WITH GANACHE AND MASCARPONE CREAM

1 cup unsalted butter (plus more for pan)
¼ cup unsweetened cocoa powder (plus more for pan)
1 ¼ cup heavy cream
8 ounces bittersweet chocolate, chopped
5 large eggs
1 cup sugar

Pre-heat the oven to 350 degrees F.
Butter a 9-inch springform pan and dust with cocoa powder.
In medium saucepan heat the butter with the ¼ cup of cream over medium low heat until the butter is melted. Add the chocolate and stir until melted and smooth. Remove from heat.
In a medium bowl whisk together the eggs, sugar, and cocoa powder. Whisk this into the chocolate mixture. Transfer the batter to the prepared pan and bake until puffed, about 35-40 minutes. Let cool in pan for 1 hour. Run knife around the edge of the cake before unmolding.

GANACHE
2/3 cup heavy cream
6 ounces semisweet chocolate, finely chopped
1 tablespoon light corn syrup

Bring cream to a boil in a small saucepan. Remove from heat and add chocolate and corn syrup. Let stand for 5 minutes. Whisk until smooth. Transfer to bowl and let cool, stirring often.

MASCARPONE CREAM

2 tablespoons boiling water
2 tablespoons Instant espresso powder
¾ cup mascarpone at room temperature
1 cup whipping cream
½ cup confectioners' sugar

Stir the water and espresso powder in a large bowl to blend. Stir in the mascarpone. Beat the cream in a large bowl while slowly adding the powdered sugar until soft peaks form. Fold one quarter of the whipped cream into the mascarpone mixture to lighten. Fold remaining whipped cream into mixture.
(Unless you plan on frosting the entire cake, only make half of this mixture to decorate or dollop on the cake.)

STRAWBERRY-RHUBARB CRUMBLE

1 cup white sugar
3 tablespoons flour
4 cups sliced strawberries
3 cups diced rhubarb
1 ½ cups flour
1 cup brown sugar
1 cup butter
1 cup rolled oats

Preheat oven to 375 degrees F (190 degrees C).
Mix white sugar, 3 tablespoons flour,
strawberries, and rhubarb--place in
a 9 x 13-inch baking dish. Mix 1 ½ cups flour,
brown sugar, butter, and oats until crumbly.
Crumble on top of the strawberry-rhubarb
mixture. Bake 45 minutes, or until crisp and
lightly browned.

KAY'S PEACH COBBLER

½ cup butter
1 cup sugar
1 ½ teaspoons baking powder
1 teaspoon salt
1 cup milk
3 cups peaches, peeled and sliced
juice of ½ lemon
¼ teaspoon ground cloves
¼ teaspoon ground nutmeg
1 cup flour

Preheat oven to 350 degrees F.

Place peaches in 9 x 13-inch baking dish and sprinkle the lemon juice on top. Place in heating oven while preparing the mixture.

Cream butter and sugar. Mix dry ingredients together and add to butter mixture. Add milk. Mix well and place on top of peaches.

Bake for 40 minutes.

Top with ice cream while hot! (Strafford ginger ice cream goes great with it!)

TIRAMISU

1 ¼ cup mascarpone
6 egg yolks
1 ¼ cup sugar
1 ¾ cup whipping cream
¾ cup hot water
2 teaspoons instant coffee/espresso
1 ½ tablespoons brandy (or more)
3 packages of ladyfingers
Grated semi-sweet chocolate

Beat egg yolks and sugar until thick and lemon colored at medium speed.
Put yolks and sugar in double boiler; Cook 8-10 minutes whisking continuously.
Remove egg yolk mixture from heat and add the mascarpone. Beat until smooth.
Beat cream and fold into the cheese mixture.
Combine water, coffee, and brandy.
Brush this mixture on the cut side of the lady fingers.
Line bottom and sides of a 3-quart trifle/souffle bowl.
Alternate cheese mixture with grated chocolate and lady fingers. Chill for 8 hours.

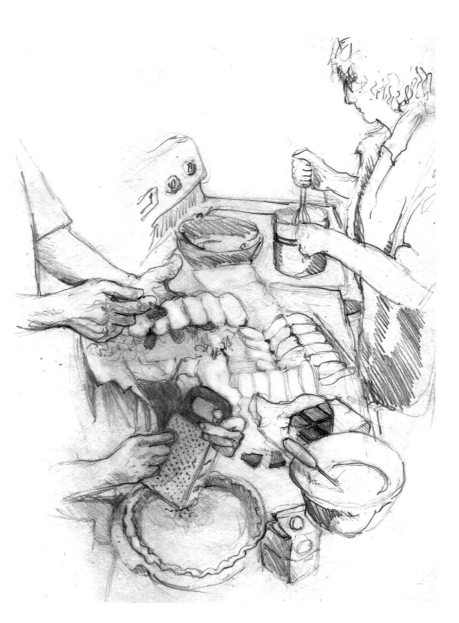

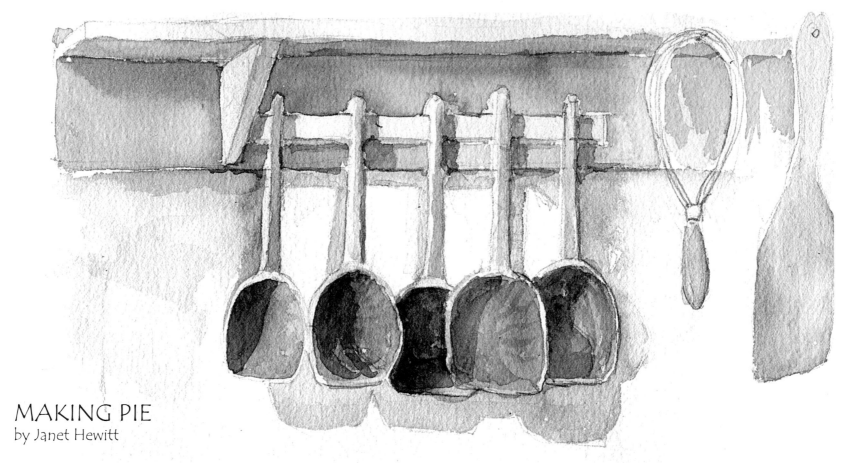

MAKING PIE
by Janet Hewitt

I'd like to make apple pie with Hayden again, hear the slow scrape of his knife circling apples, coils of skin dropping to the table, while I push the rolling pin across pastry. I'd tell him again, as we work, how my mother used only lard in her crusts and she always took home empty tins from church suppers; people knew. I'd remind him this was the fourth kitchen he'd been in of mine, and my favorite was the first, even with its sloping floor and drafty doors.

How come, I'd ask him, we remember discomfort with so much affection? Then I'd stop talking, if I had a chance to make pie with Hayden again, and allow the silence to hold us and our work of scraping and rolling, the way I felt held that cold January morning twenty years ago, making pie with him in the fourth kitchen, a silence so intense and lovely, I leaned way, way back into it, and rested there, in that perfection, with my friend.

JANA'S CRUNCHY OATMEAL COOKIES

½ cup brown sugar
½ cup sugar
2 sticks (1 cup) butter
1 teaspoon cinnamon
1 teaspoon baking soda
2 eggs
1 ½ cups flour
2 cups rolled oats
½ to 1 teaspoon salt
1 cup chopped pecans
1 tablespoon apple cider vinegar

For lighter cookies substitute 1 cup of sugar for the sugars above.

Cream sugar and butter, then add other ingredients. Add vinegar as the last ingredient to the mixture. Drop by teaspoonfuls onto cookie sheet and take fork tines dipped in water and mash. Bake in 375 degree F oven for 8 to 10 minutes.

This makes a very crunchy cookie (the vinegar is the secret) and was my mother's favorite cookie.

OATMEAL LACE COOKIES
with Janet Ancel and Olivia Gay

Oatmeal lace cookies were among the rarest and most desirable foods to come out of our grandmother's kitchen. Louise Andrews Kent was the co-author with our mother, Elizabeth Kent Gay, of "The Winter Kitchen," and these cookies made their appearance in that cookbook on page 110. This version of the recipe is attributed to Pearl Bullock, who helped Grandma in her Kents' Corner kitchen for many years.

Louise Andrews Kent wrote as Mrs. Appleyard and our mother took the name Cicely Bradshaw. Janet and I were Jane and Camilla Bradshaw, respectively, and Pearl, Elaine Fitch's aunt, became Patience Barlow.

"The Winter Kitchen" and its companion, "The Summer Kitchen," wove recipes throughout the re-telling of events with family, friends, and community. In this case, the cookies were made for the party following the Christmas Eve candlelight service at the Old West Church. In the early years, Forest and Betty Davis (Fair and Eleanor Davenport in the book) invited everyone to their house for refreshments and the ritual lighting of real candles on their Christmas tree. I can recall in detail the massive tree with its flickering lights, the scent of spruce mixed with the house warmth after the cold church, and the table spread with seasonal treats, a big plate of crisp oatmeal lace cookies among them.

Janet and I remember there was a strict limit of two per child, to accompany vanilla ice cream topped with raspberries served in Grandma's dining room in the White House

in Kents' Corner I still have the dining table they were served upon, and Janet still has the orange Reed's Butter-scotch tin where the cookies were kept between layers of wax paper. We both remember stealing into the pantry to carefully open the tin and quietly rustle the wax paper to find the buttery burnt sugar disks, pop one in our mouths, and race out before detection. Did Grandma know of our thievery? If she did, I'm sure it was an amusement to her. When you read the recipe in "The Winter Kitchen," you will get a sense of the mystique that surrounded the baking of the cookies. The day should be clear with high barometric pressure so the cookies don't stick on their prescribed heavy metal pans greased once with butter. After a precise 7 minutes in the oven, the cookies must stand exactly one minute to be peeled gently off the pan but not left too long or they would adhere in a hard crunchy mass. The oats must be regular, not quick, the brown sugar light not dark, the recipe made in its entirety unless you beat the egg, measure it, and use half of it. A messy business and what do you do with what's left? Throw it away? Not in New England'. (p. 112, "The Winter Kitchen").

Janet remembers making them for the first time after Grandma died in 1969. She and her mother-in-law, Susan Ancel, approached the baking anxiously, wondering if the day was right, the pans heavy enough, the timer working properly. They quickly realized that the batter itself is the easy part since it is made in a single saucepan. Once the batter was made, they went on to several hours of keeping two cookie pans going and gingerly approaching the cookies as they came out of the oven bubbling with sugar. This first attempt was a modest success, and Janet went on : to innovate in ways that would have certainly surprised Grandma, and most likely brought a smile of wry approval: using parchment paper to make for easy-release cookies, buying a large pan to make a dozen at a time, refrigerating the batter to make them on her own schedule, and finally packing them in a plastic container that keeps them fresh for weeks rather than days. But Janet never, ever messes with the ingredients even though she sometimes makes the cookies on days with middling barometric pressure. She also admits that once she made a half batch and they turned out fine.

For myself, after Grandma was gone, it was a revelation that I could make oatmeal lace cookies whenever I wanted, frequently giving them away as Christmas treats to neighbors. And I could eat as many as I wanted, always remembering Grandma when I had that first meltingly sweet taste of a rich glassy cookie 'of a golden lacy color and texture that Benvenuto Cellini might have equaled if he'd felt in the mood and had enough gold on hand'. (p. 110, "The Winter Kitchen")

Recipe

Preheat over to 375 degrees F
1 cup butter, melted
2 ¼ cups light brown sugar
1 tablespoon white sugar
2 ¼ cups regular rolled oats
1 tablespoon white flour
1 egg slightly beaten
1 teaspoon vanilla

In a saucepan large enough to hold the whole mixture, melt the butter over low heat. When it starts to froth a little, stir in the sugars, brown and white. Remove the pan from the heat. Stir in the oats and the flour. Let the mixture cool for at least 5 minutes. This is important. Add the beaten egg and vanilla. Set the mixture in a cool place while the oven is heating. In the meantime cut and place parchment paper to fit the pan(s).

Put the mixture on the pan by teaspoonfuls, pushing it off the spoon in small circular lumps, leaving plenty of room for the cookies to spread. Fill a second pan as soon as the first is in the oven. It takes 5-7 minutes to bake them.

Watch them carefully. They should be deep golden brown on the edges.
Let them stand on the pan for a minute or two and remove to cool individually and completely before storing in a tightly covered container between sheets of waxed paper 'and try to hide it from your grandchildren till dinnertime. p. 113, "The Winter Kitchen")
This recipe, with Janet's innovations, makes 150-180 cookies. That's more than enough to allow 2 per child, maybe even 3 or 4.

HELEN'S TROPICAL GALETTE

Helen wrote down these instructions from memory and she hasn't had time to make the galette since she did that, so proceed at your own risk. If it turns out great, enjoy! If it is a disaster, try to figure out what went wrong and let us know the next time you drop by the store. Helen says it is good with ice cream . . . and rum . . . so, really, is there any risk it will be bad?

Dough:
1-1/3 cups all purpose flour
1/4 teaspoon salt
2 tablespoons confectioners sugar
8 tablespoons (1 stick) cold unsalted butter, cut into pieces
1 egg

Filling:
1/3 cup dark chocolate chips
3 generous tablespoons raspberry jam
Approximately 3 bananas, peeled and sliced into thick coins
1/2 cup unsweetened coconut flakes
1/3 cup brown sugar
1/2 cup chopped toasted pecans or hazelnuts
4 tablespoons butter
Cinnamon
Cream (optional)

Combine flour, salt, and sugar in food processor, pulse a few times. Add butter and pulse until combined, sort of like thick cornmeal. Add egg and pulse until just combined.

Remove dough, press into thick disk, wrap in plastic wrap, and refrigerate for 30 minutes.

Preheat oven to 400 degrees F. On a floured surface, roll the dough into a circle about 12-14 inches in diameter (don't make the crust too thin or it will collapse under the weight of the filling). Transfer to a greased cookie sheet (if it overhangs a little that's okay because you're going to be folding the edge in).

To make the filling, microwave together (or heat in a small saucepan over low heat) the chocolate and raspberry jam until smooth. Spread evenly onto dough, leaving a 1-2 inch rim unchocolated. Cover chocolate with bananas.

In a small saucepan, melt together the butter and brown sugar, add in the coconut and nuts, and stir until everything is coated. Spread over bananas. Sprinkle with cinnamon.

Fold over the unchocolated rim of the dough to cover the edges of the tart--it can be sloppy. Brush with cream (optional). Then bake for about 30 minutes. I recommend starting on a lower rack for the first part of baking. The crust should be dark brown--you don't want it to burn, but you also want it fairly sturdy.

Remove from oven. DO NOT try to remove from the sheet until it is completely cooled. It will be tempting and you WILL regret it.

VICTORIA'S STOUT CAKE

Moving to a new community is never easy, but moving to the Adamant community was perhaps the easiest transition we've had as a family. Our choice to come onto the family land that our ancestors lived on, and the house my son's grandmother grew up in was a homecoming of large and small dreams realized: To live on workable farmland; to live rural; to live in a place where we could leave our doors unlocked and our hearts open to the idiosyncrasies of this small enclave of strong women and fabulous food-- a community rich with story; with activity; with food grown, cooked, preserved, and eaten.

My four year-old son; Forrest, has taken most sweetly to weekly visits to the Co-op, where we purchase small treats and sit by the stove in winter, or play in the stream across the road in summer. Community and sweet things always make him smile, and sharing that sweetness with friends, particularly when we make a good thing together, makes him most happy. In our rural home, we don't have a television, but we pepper our days outside and with books and the occasional cooking video on the computer. He usually elects to watch a confection or cake tutorial, and this put us in a good position to rise to the occasion of the Adamant Co-op's call for confections for the annual Valentine's Day Dessert and Wine Tasting event.

The following recipe for Chocolate Stout Cake with Chocolate Ganache and Chocolate Coconut Curls came

about by pulling from various recipes and consulting with our tastebuds. Forrest helped perfect the dish and participated with great restraint in anticipation of having a slice at the event. Although many people thronged the dessert table at the co-op that evening, my son and I could be found seated near the door, diligently tasting the cake we spent hours working on together. He often tells me, though we've cooked and eaten many a confection since then, that his favorite cake is the chocolate stout cake we made together in February of 2014. So enjoy, and know this cake tastes best if made with a child under 6.

A quick note about ingredients: we chose to make this cake coffee free. Other recipes call for ½ cup of black coffee, but we used more stout. It's up to you-- the taste is rich either way.

For the cake:
2 cups Gritty McDuff Black Fly Stout
2 sticks (1 cup) unsalted butter
1 ½ cups unsweetened cocoa powder
4 cups all purpose flour
4 cups sugar
1 tablespoon. baking soda
1 ½ teaspoons salt
4 eggs
1-1/3 cup sour cream

For the filling:
1 cup heavy cream
½ teaspoon vanilla
¼ cup sugar

For the Icing:
2 cups heavy cream
½ pound. semi-sweet chocolate
½ pound. bittersweet chocolate, at least 70% cocoa
2 tablespoons. coconut oil

For the chocolate curls:
6 ounces. bittersweet chocolate, at least 70% cocoa
3 tablespoons coconut oil

Order of operations:
1. Cake mix
2. Coconut curl preparation
3. Ganache
4. Whipped cream
5. Assembly

Cake

1. Preheat the oven to 350 degrees F. Make sure there is enough room for four cake pans in the middle of the oven. Prepare four 8-inch circular pans with butter and a dusting of cocoa powder. You can also use parchment on the bottom of the pan, as this is pretty darn sticky stuff.
2. Melt butter with the stout. Add cocoa powder, whisk together, and remove from heat to cool.
3. Whisk or sift together flour, sugar, salt, and baking soda.
4. Mix together eggs, sour cream, and vanilla in a separate bowl--your biggest one. Add cooled stout, cocoa, and butter mixture, mix together, and then add in a few steps the dry mixture. Don't over mix, it doesn't have to be clump free.
5. Divide batter into the four pans. Cook for about 20 minutes in center of oven, until there is no batter on a chopstick inserted into the center of the cake.
Cool in pan for 10 minutes, then turn out on racks or whatever you have to completely cool. COMPLETELY cool.

Coconut Chocolate Curls

1. Melt over double boiler 6 ounces of bittersweet chocolate and 3 tablespoons of coconut oil.
2. Once it's all melted, spread liquid chocolate on the back of a cookie pan or other flat surface. Make this layer maybe

1/8- to 1/4-inch thick.
3. Cool completely in refrigerator until it's solid again. Maybe 20 minutes, tops.
4. Using a knife or sharp spatula, push into the layer of chocolate at an angle and run it along the flat bottom of the cookie sheet. Tight curls of chocolate will be formed.
5. If for some reason they are flaking (too cold) or not curling (too warm), play with the temperature of the chocolate--leave it for a minute out of the refrigerator or put it back in to cool it. Try again.
6. Store curls in the refrigerator until assembly.

Icing

1. Heat heavy cream just below a boil. Remove from heat.
2. Immediately add oil and chocolate. Stir to melt and combine completely.
3. Place in fridge until completely cool, stirring every 20 minutes or so. This can take up to an hour or more. Do not let it become too stiff, as it becomes difficult to spread on the cake.

Whipped Cream Filling

1. Place very cold whipping cream in a wide cool bowl. Add sugar and vanilla.
2. Whip with electric mixer (unless you are being burly and do it by hand) until stiff peaks form--not butter(!) but stiff peaks.

Assembly

1. Place one cake layer down. Add enough whipped cream to cover top of cake, leaving a ¼ inch around lip so cream doesn't spill over.
2. Place second cake layer on. Repeat with whipped cream.

3. Third layer. Whipped cream. Remember 1/4 inch lip of no cream.
4. Fourth layer. Wow that's tall.
5. Apply icing, starting at the sides. I choose to start at the sides and build up so as to make sure there is enough to cover sides. Ice all sides of cake.
6. Put chocolate curls on top of cake, and place wherever you would like--spilling along the side, around the base, whatever suits you.
7. Enjoy!

This cake can last a day or so in the fridge--longer if it's in a sealed container. It tastes best if it's at room temperature.

LARRY'S CLAFOUTI

3 cups pitted dark (sweet) cherries
¼ cup kirsch, cognac, or brandy
1/3 cup sugar

Add liqueur and sugar to cherries and let stand for an hour. Gently stir occasionally.

For the batter:
1 cup milk
1/3 cup sugar
3 eggs
1 tablespoon vanilla
pinch of salt
2/3 cup all-purpose flour

Preheat the oven to 350 degrees F. Butter a 7- to 8-cup, 1 ½ inch deep baking dish, pie plate, or seasoned cast-iron skillet.

Drain the cherries and reserve the liquid. Place milk, about ¼ cup of reserved liquid, sugar, eggs, vanilla, and salt in the jar of a blender and blend carefully. With blender running, add the flour. Blend for a minute or two.

Pour a layer of the batter (about ¼ inch deep) into prepared dish. Put in the oven until the batter begins to set. Remove from the oven and add the cherries (spreading them evenly across the dish). Pour the remainder of the batter on top and let it settle around the cherries. Put back into the oven and bake for about one hour (the

clafouti is done when it is evenly browned and a knife plunged into the center comes back clean).

Dust clafouti with powdered sugar and serve warm.

PEANUT BUTTER FROSTING FOR CHOCOLATE CAKE

1. Make your favorite chocolate cake recipe.
2. Frost with Peanut Butter Frosting:
Ingredients:
1/3 cup butter, softened
1 cup creamy peanut butter
3 ¾ cup confectioners' sugar
1 teaspoon vanilla
Add 3-4 tablespoons milk as needed to make it spreadable.
Beat butter and peanut butter together until smooth. Add sugar, vanilla, and milk gradually, alternating for easier mixing.

BRAZDALONE ITALIAN CAKE

… a simple recipe and oh so good. My father's cousin, Carrie, made this every Christmas.
-       Jane B. Wass

1 ½ cups sugar
¼ pound butter
3 whole eggs beaten
1 teaspoon almond extract
1 teaspoon vanilla extract
2 ½ cups flour
1 cup raisins
Chopped maraschino cherries (amount to your liking)
Grated zest of ½ lemon

Cream together 1 ½ cups sugar with ¼ pound butter.
Break 3 whole eggs into the creamed mixture and beat.
Add 1 teaspoon (each) vanilla and almond extract to the mix and blend.
Add 2 ½ cups sifted flour with 2 teaspoons baking powder (batter will be very stiff).
Add 1 cup raisins and a few chopped cherries and lemon zest.
Sprinkle top with sugar before baking.

Bake in greased baking tin (I use a bread pan, but you can use an angel food tin as well).
Bake at 350 degrees F for 50 minutes or until a toothpick comes out clean.

ERIN'S PASTA FLORA (APRICOT JAM PASTRY)

Pre heat oven to 350 degrees F

1 cup butter, softened
¾ cup granulated sugar
2 eggs
2 ounces brandy
3 ½ cups flour
2 teaspoons baking powder
1 ½ pounds of apricot preserves
1 ounce brandy (optional)
1 egg yolk
2 tablespoons water

Cream butter and sugar. Add eggs and beat well. Add 2 ounces brandy. Sift dry ingredients into butter mixture and mix well. Add enough flour so the dough is not sticky. Press two thirds of the dough into a 9 x 13-inch pan, including up the sides. Mix preserves and additional ounce of brandy and spread evenly over dough. Roll out remaining one third of the dough about ¼-inch thick and slice into strips, place over the apricot preserves in a lattice design. Brush entire pastry with beaten egg yolk and water. Sprinkle top with granulated sugar, bake at 350 degrees F for 20 minutes or until lightly brown.

HUBBA HUBBA BURNIN' LOVE COOKIES

1 cup sugar
½ cup butter
1 egg
1 teaspoon vanilla
1 ¼ cups white flour
½ cup dark chocolate cocoa powder (I assume regular cocoa powder would work, but I liked the dark chocolate version)
1 ½ teaspoons baking powder
½ teaspoon cayenne pepper
½ teaspoon cinnamon
1 teaspoon chili powder
½ cup dark chocolate chips

Beat in a standing mixer the sugar and butter, minus 1 tablespoon. Beat until light and creamy. While this is beating, mix dry ingredients in a bowl.
Melt chocolate and 1 tablespoon butter together in the microwave. Add to sugar/butter mixture and be sure it's well incorporated.
Add egg and vanilla, then slowly add dry ingredients. Cover and chill in the refrigerator for 12–24 hours (or don't, frankly I say take a few hunks of dough and bake some early cookies to tide you over).
Heat the oven to 350 degrees F. On a lightly floured surface roll dough until it's a pretty generous cookie thickness (about 1/3 inch). Cut out with heart cutters and bake 10-12 minutes. If you use dark cocoa powder it's really hard to tell doneness by color--tap the top and it should be firm but still soft when you take them out. After the cookies have cooled, mix 1 cup of confectioner's sugar, red food coloring, and as much milk as you need (hardly any) to make a thick glaze. Frost the cookies.

BETTY DAVIS'S ADAMANT ZUCCHINI CHOCOLATE CAKE

Ingredients:
1 package Adamant Mostly Local Chocolate Cake Mix
1 package Adamant Mostly Local Fudge Brownie Mix
1 cup water
4 eggs
¾ cup milk
1 cup oil
2 cups of grated zucchini

Preheat the oven to 350 degrees F. Boil water.
Beat eggs well, add milk, oil, and zucchini; blend.
Add chocolate cake mix, beat until blended.
Add boiling water and stir briefly. Add fudge brownie mix and blend.
Bake in 13 x 9 x 2-inch pan for 45 minutes.

DONNA'S CARROT CAKE WITH CREAM CHEESE PEANUT BUTTER FROSTING

1. Make your favorite carrot cake recipe. (I just pick one from on-line, not sure I have the best one yet).
2. Frost with Cream Cheese Peanut Butter Frosting:
Ingredients:
¾ cup creamy peanut butter
8 ounces softened cream cheese
3 ¾ cup confectioners' sugar (about 1 box)
1 teaspoon vanilla

Add milk as needed to make it spreadable.
Beat peanut butter and cream cheese together until smooth. Add sugar, vanilla, and milk gradually, alternating for easier mixing.

This is enough to frost a 13 x 9-inch cake including the sides if it has been removed from the pan.
It is good sprinkled with chopped pecans unless you are decorating it for a birthday cake.

TORTA DELLA NONNA

There are perhaps as many recipes for this torta (cake) as there are nonnas (grandmothers) in Italy--each has her own, and to her family it is the best. This particular one has appeared as a dessert at Friday Night Cookouts at the Co-op. The pastry is particularly difficult to work with. It is soft and crumbles easily and there may be times you want to throw it out the window, but stick with it and try not to worry too much about how it looks.

For the Pastry:
2 cups flour
1 egg
2 egg yolks
½ cup sugar
3 tablespoons unsalted butter
3 tablespoons extra virgin olive oil
½ teaspoon vanilla extract
½ teaspoon salt

For the Filling:
2 cups fresh whole-milk ricotta cheese
½ cup pine nuts
½ cup sugar
Zest and juice of 1 lemon
3 eggs

Preheat the oven to 350 degrees F.
Melt together the butter and olive oil and allow to cool. Mound the two cups of flour on a pastry board or a clean counter and make a well in the center of the flour. Put the egg, egg yolks, butter-and-olive-oil mixture, sugar, and vanilla in the well. Using a fork, carefully stir the wet ingredients and bring the flour little by little into the well and mix with the wet ingredients until the mixture is thick enough to allow you to use your hands to form it into a dough. Knead until smooth and elastic. Allow the dough to rest at least 15 minutes. Chill it in the refrigerator if necessary.

Make the filling by beating together the ricotta, pine nuts, sugar, lemon zest and juice, and eggs, until smooth. Divide the dough so that one portion is slightly larger than the other. Roll the larger portion of dough to form a 12- to 13-inch circle and place it on the bottom of a 9-inch tart ring with a removable bottom (you can also use a 9-inch cake pan, a 9-inch pie plate, or a 9-inch spring form pan, whichever works best for you). Carefully work the dough up the sides of the pan so you have enough to pinch together with the top (you may have to press and patch the dough in the bottom to make it cover and fit) Roll the second portion of dough into a 10- to 11-inch circle. Spread the ricotta mixture evenly over the bottom of the pan and place the remaining circle of dough over the top and pinch the edges of the top and bottom together. Bake for 35 to 40 minutes. Can be served warm or at room temperature.

CREAM TEA

Every autumn for the past few years, during peak foliage season, we have offered traditional cream teas at Janet's studio, which is on the second floor of the Co-op. The atmosphere is unbeatable: imagine yourself sitting in Janet's studio, surrounded by her art, sun streaming in, Sodom Pond glittering in the sun, the trees seemingly on fire, drinking tea and eating still-warm scones with clotted cream and strawberry jam.

TRADITIONAL CREAM SCONES
Yield: 9 medium

Preheat oven to 400 degrees F

2 cups flour
1 tablespoon baking powder
pinch of salt
2 tablespoons sugar
5 tablespoons COLD butter, chopped into small pieces
1 cup heavy cream--reserve about 1 tablespoon for brushing on top

Optional: raisins, cranberries, currants, blueberries, chopped dried apricots, small amounts of real extracts such as orange, almond, lemon

Put flour, baking powder, salt, and sugar in bowl of a food processor with the regular steel blade and pulse briefly. Add butter and pulse until mixture feels like crumb topping.
With the processor running, gradually stream in all of the cream except for 1 tablespoon. (If you want to add flavoring add it to the cream). Keep blending until mixture begins to clump and thump. Lightly flour cutting board and dump mixture onto it. It may look a bit clumpy and crumbly. Don't worry. That's how it's supposed to look. Quickly, handling as little as possible, knead a few times just to bring everything together.
Roll to about 3/4 inch thickness. (If you want to add fruit, roll it thinner, press the fruit in, fold in half and roll briefly.

Using a water glass of any size you want (this assumes you don't have cookie cutters), cut out dough circles and place on baking sheet lined with parchment paper. Keep reconsolidating dough and cutting until you've used it all. Brush tops with reserved cream.

Bake for about 15-20 minutes, until tops are lightly speckled golden brown.

Consume ravenously plain or with clotted cream and jam, or butter. These freeze beautifully.

CLOTTED CREAM

There are many ways to make clotted cream. We have found the following technique to be one of the easier ways to make it--and it tastes really good.

Get a bottle of good quality cream. Take a cast iron skillet and pour the cream into it. Put the skillet on your stove on very low heat. Spoon the film that forms on the surface of the cream into a jar, keep doing this until all the cream is gone. Put the clotted cream into the refrigerator and enjoy it with scones. (It is also very good on pancakes!)

VANILLA PASTRY CREAM

This is for incredible Italian pastry cream-fruit parfaits

2 cups any kind of milk
½ vanilla bean (real vanilla beans make a huge difference, but if you can't find them, use 1-2 teaspoons really good quality vanilla extract
6 egg yolks
2/3 cup granulated sugar
¼ cup cornstarch
1 tablespoon butter
Fresh blueberries, strawberries, blackberries. I suppose you could use frozen if desperate.
1 cup heavy cream, whipped to stiff peaks.

Pour the milk into a medium sauce pan. Scrape out inside of vanilla bean and add it plus the bean to the milk. Bring to a boil, making sure not to burn the bottom. Set aside and allow the bean to soak in the milk for another 15 minutes before removing.

Beat egg yolks and sugar until light and fluffy. Add cornstarch and beat some more until smooth.

Whisk in ¼ cup of the milk mixture. If it's still hot whisk fast enough to make sure you don't get scrambled vanilla eggs. Whisk in the rest of the milk.

Pour back into pan and cook over medium-high heat, stirring constantly until thick and gently bubbling.

Take off of heat and add butter.
Let cool slightly. Then cover with plastic wrap, pressing it down against the custard to keep it from making a skin. Chill for 2 hours or more.

When cool, fold in whipped cream.

Take some beautiful wine glasses and alternate layers of pastry cream and fruit. Position fruit so you can see it through the glasses and save some for the top.

Chill until ready to serve.

APFELSTRUDEL

My sister and I always looked forward to visiting my grandmother. She spoiled us rotten, told wonderful stories of her own childhood, and sometimes heartbreaking stories of life in Vienna during World War II -- and she always made amazing food. One of our favorites was Apfelstrudel. My Oma said that a friend of hers who owned a café once told her that the dough for a strudel has to be so thin that you can read a newspaper through it. Good luck with that!

Ingredients

For the dough:
250 grams (1 cup) flour
pinch of salt
2 tablespoons canola oil
1 egg
1 tablespoon vinegar
flour for the work surface

For the filling:
1.5 kilograms (about 3 pounds) apples
4 tablespoons sugar
2 teaspoons ground cinnamon
3 tablespoons raisins
100 grams (6 tablespoons) butter
100 grams (½ cup) breadcrumbs
4 teaspoons sour cream

Confectioner's sugar for decoration

Pre-heat oven to 180 degrees C (350 degrees F)

Sift the flour and salt onto a work surface. Make a dent in the middle and add 1 tablespoon oil, the egg, and the vinegar. Slowly add 100 milliliters (about 6 ½ table-spoons) of lukewarm water. Mix together until the mixture turns into dough. Form into a ball. Cover dough and let rest for 30 minutes.

In the meantime, peel and thinly slice the apples. Add sugar, cinnamon, and raisins. Melt half the butter and brown the breadcrumbs. Set aside. Melt the remaining butter.

Cover a baking sheet with wax paper. Cut the dough in half. Take a kitchen towel, sprinkle it with flour, and roll the dough out on it. Use your hands to pull it out until it is very thin.

Baste dough with melted butter, add half the sour cream, half the breadcrumb mixture, and half the apples. With the help of the kitchen towel fold up the strudel and carefully transfer it to the baking sheet. Repeat with second dough. Baste both strudels with butter and bake in the oven for 35 to 40 minutes (until the strudel is golden brown). After 20 minutes in the oven, baste with the remaining melted butter. Before serving, sprinkle with confectioner's sugar.

My Adamant
by Janet Pocorobba

The rises of the roads are in me now.
Who can forget
that flaking silo at the bend in the road,
the forest where I saw a deer scare
her fawn back to safety?
The crossroads dip down, heart high,
view of Holsteins and Angus.
Two men take out a canoe.
Layers of purple and green
hills in soft
mellow rises
C cups, no bigger, B maybe or A's.
My kind of place,
gentle swells but many,
like interlocking fingers, a congregation,
conversation, heads together at a meeting.
Bodies sleeping next to each other.
Slumbering hills, easy and wide, like a mother's embrace,
a woman's thighs
saying: rest.
Rest here.

The Doorway to Adamant
by Larry Floersch

The warped clapboards of the barn and the staves of the silos of the old farm give no hint of the color they might have been painted when new, if they ever were painted or ever were new. The farmhouse, too, is badly weathered, white paint pulling back from gray wood, like an early snow on a gravel road. The squat Ford tractor is from the 1940s, and on rare occasions when a barn door is open, you can glimpse a Model A inside, maybe purchased new and only driven on Sundays. It is a farm from another century or perhaps the one before, and it signals to travelers on this road a change in how time moves.

The road leading to the old farm from the south is wide, with vistas of the Winooski valley and the mountains beyond Plainfield as it rises and falls back to Montpelier just a few miles distant—so close that on a quiet evening if you listen you can hear the commotion of the town folk--train whistles at the junction or the occasional siren. But Montpelier runs on human time—minutes, weeks, months, legislative fiscal years. Here at this barnyard, time changes to farm time, where the rhythm of the cows is paramount and the seasons dictate chores. The cows do not know of weeks, and the chickens could care less about daylight saving time. For all the years I have returned from the human world in Burlington or Waterbury or Montpelier along this road, it is here at the old farm and the woods just beyond where I allow the artificiality of human time to fall away and I again embrace the spinning of the natural world.

I always downshift and slow as I approach, partly because the road rises and blindly bends to the right at the barnyard, and partly because, if it is late afternoon, the road may be filled by a small herd of Jerseys crossing from the

upper pasture to the barn, anxious to get to the milking machine and their supper. Arrive a bit earlier and the cows will be milling unbidden at the pasture gate, waiting for their humans to allow them safe passage to the barnyard, and as certain of the time, their time, as if they each had a Lady Rolex strapped above a fetlock. A farm is a community unto itself, the inhabitants—human and other—self-reliant but relying on each other.

Just past the old farm the woods close in and the road rises again and pinches down to a single lane. Ancient maples line the road here, so close they bear scars of many winters' plowing and their boughs intermingle and arch into a canopy. A "tree tunnel," my grandson calls it, but more of a cathedral nave, really, or the great hall through which Dorothy and her friends walked as they approached Oz the Great and Powerful, she in the ruby slippers she had yet to control. A hundred yards or so and the road widens again, but just barely enough to allow two vehicles to pass. Things feel different now. A portal has opened and closed and I have passed through. The urge to accelerate is gone. Time has slowed. Clocks are meaningless. I feel the rhythm of the cows.

Two miles farther on, the road ends altogether at the steps of the Adamant Co-op. Like the old farm, the Co-op too is from another century, and like the old farm it runs at its own pace and generates its own community, a community that reaches as far as the portal at the farm. At the Co-op the merchandise proclaims, "All Roads Lead to Adamant," and it is true that several roads converge before it. Adamant can be reached from several directions, but to me only one road, Center Road, has the old farm guarding the cathedral of maples that are the doorway to Adamant, the portal to home. Ruby slippers are not required.

A NOTE ABOUT SOURCES

One of the joys of needing to eat is that we have to procure the edibles first. That is half the fun. Whether you are shopping at your local cooperative or your hometown farmers' market, you may cross paths with or buy direct from the producer of your next meal. What better way to get fresh food, product information. At the Adamant Co-op we try to work together and buy from one another whenever possible, whether it be eggs, maple syrup, honey, or beef. Local sources mean local control and the money stays local. Keeping the money local helps your neighbors.

We urge anyone using this book to consider buying as local as possible. Start with your local farmers' market if you have one and work your way out from there to find what you need, be it in your town or city, county or state. We'll all be better off for it.

Here is a list of local sources in the Adamant area:

ART, JEWELRY, POTTERY, CARDS, CALENDARS:

Janet MacLeod (223-2296): paintings, prints, cards, and, last but not least, wonderful papier mâché animals
Linda Fisher (Linspired, 223-3726): pottery
Linda Schutz (Ancient Woman Pottery, 229-6861): pottery
Paige Canfield (Carve Design, carvedesignsvt.com): cards, calendars
Erika Mitchell (456-7054): cards, prints, CDs
Gary Lewis (223-5760): cards
Eric Ryea (223-5760): cards
Sage Zelkowitz (sagesmedicine@wildmail.com): cards
Jane Wass (229-1065): seamstress extraordinaire

Regina Thompson (Spinning Head Studios, 223-8483): jewelry, cards, prints

BEAUTY PRODUCTS:

Elmore Mountain Farm (elmoremountainfarm.com. 802-888-8585): soap, bug repellant, body care products

FOOD:

Colin Blackwell (279-5522): garlic, produce
Peck Family Farm, Dan and Leila Bair (223-3023): maple syrup, pumpkins, cider apples
Templeton Farm, Bruce and Janet Chapell (223-0169, templetonfarm.com): maple syrup, grass-fed beef
Manghi's Bread (223-3676): bread, rolls, hot crossed buns, other seasonal baked goods
Rick Barstow (223-3311): maple syrup
Franklin Heyburn (225-6051): honey
Open Way Farm, Victoria Pearson (223-2324): produce
Fox Run Farm, Tom and Sandal Cate (223-6466): eggs, honey, produce
Leatherwood Farm, Karen Lieberman (223-6277): eggs
Cindy Gardner-Morse (223-5738): eggs
Patchwork Farm and Bakery (patchworkfarmbakery.com): bread
Butterworks Farm (butterworksfarm.com): yoghurt, cream, kefir, flour
Wise Owl Bakery, Marisa Keller (wiseowlbakery@gmail.com): cookies, scones, cakes
Valentine Farm, Megan Cannella (802-881-1645, valentinefarmvt@gmail.com): potatoes

INDEX